S. Hrg. 115–105

RUSSIAN INTERVENTION IN EUROPEAN ELECTIONS

HEARING

BEFORE THE

SELECT COMMITTEE ON INTELLIGENCE

OF THE

UNITED STATES SENATE

ONE HUNDRED FIFTEENTH CONGRESS

FIRST SESSION

WEDNESDAY, JUNE 28, 2017

Printed for the use of the Select Committee on Intelligence

Available via the World Wide Web: http://www.fdsys.gov

U.S. GOVERNMENT PUBLISHING OFFICE

26–127 PDF   WASHINGTON : 2017

CONTENTS

RUSSIAN INTERVENTION IN EUROPEAN ELECTIONS

WEDNESDAY, JUNE 28, 2017

U.S. Senate,
Select Committee on Intelligence,
Washington, DC.

The Committee met, pursuant to notice, at 10:07 a.m. in Room SH–216, Hart Senate Office Building, Hon. Richard Burr (Chairman of the Committee) presiding.

Committee Members Present: Senators Burr (presiding), Warner, Risch, Rubio, Collins, Blunt, Lankford, Cotton, Cornyn, McCain, Feinstein, Wyden, Heinrich, King, Manchin, Harris, and Reed.

OPENING STATEMENT OF HON. RICHARD BURR, CHAIRMAN, A U.S. SENATOR FROM NORTH CAROLINA

Chairman Burr. I'd like to call the hearing to order.

Today, the Committee convenes its seventh open hearing of 2017 to examine Russian interference in the 2016 U.S. elections, and the twelfth open hearing this year.

To date, our open hearings have largely focused on the domestic impact of Russia's activities. Today's witnesses, however, will highlight for the Committee and for the American people Russia's interference in the European elections. We hope to gain additional understanding of Russian efforts to undermine democratic institutions worldwide as the Committee continues its inquiry.

The Intelligence Committee assessed in January that Moscow will apply lessons learned from its campaign aimed at the United States presidential election to further influence efforts worldwide. It further assessed that Russia has sought to influence elections across Europe. Director of National Intelligence Coats echoed those words as recently as May when he testified before the Senate that Russia is seeking to influence elections in Europe, including France, Germany and the United Kingdom.

The intelligence community assesses that the Russian messaging strategy blends covert intelligence operations such as cyber activity with overt efforts by Russian government agencies, state-funded media, third-party intermediaries, and paid social media users, or trolls. Russia is employing a whole-of-government approach to undermining democratic institutions globally.

Facing down Russia's malicious activity is no longer just a bipartisan issue. To successfully protect our institutions and the integrity of our electoral systems, we must work as a global community to share our experience. Collective awareness of Moscow's inten-

(1)

tions spanning borders and continents will help us to enhance our security measures and thwart these disinformation campaigns.

Just as Germany is learning from the recent events in France and Montenegro, we will lean on our allies to inform our approach of the 2018 elections. We must advance more quickly than our adversaries and only together will we do so.

I'd like to welcome our distinguished witnesses today: Ambassador Nick Burns, the Roy and Barbara Goodman Family Professor of the Practice of Diplomacy and International Relations at Harvard Kennedy School of Government. Nick, that's a mighty long title there that you've got. We're delighted to have you.

Janis Sarts, Director of NATO's Strategic Communications Center of Excellence. Hopefully, I'm getting these names right. I'm trying my best.

Ambassador Vesko Garcevic, Professor of the Practice of Diplomacy and International Relations at Boston University Frederick Pardee School of Global Studies.

And Constanze Stelzenmueller, the inaugural Robert Bosch Senior Fellow in the Brookings Institute Center on United States and Europe.

Thank you all four for being here to help us better understand Russia's activities and the underlying intentions that Russia might have.

With that, I will turn to the Vice Chairman.

OPENING STATEMENT OF HON. MARK R. WARNER, A U.S. SENATOR FROM VIRGINIA

Vice Chairman WARNER. Thank you, Mr. Chairman. And let me commend you on your—on your brilliant introduction of our witnesses. And welcome, witnesses.

Today's hearing continues the Committee's efforts to address the issues surrounding Russia's active interference in our democratic process and in the 2016 elections here in America, as well as Russia's similar and in some cases ongoing efforts to undermine democratic institutions amongst many of our closest allies.

At this point, I believe we have a pretty good understanding of the Russian playbook. Russia's goal is to sow chaos and confusion, to fuel internal disagreements, and to undermine democracies whenever possible, really to basically cast doubt on the democratic process wherever it exists.

There's nothing unusual about Russia's scheming to influence the American elections. We all know their efforts date back to the Cold War. But Russia's blatant interference in the United States' 2016 presidential elections was unprecedented in both scale and scope.

And we've seen it replicated across Europe. In fact, Russia's active measures are only growing bolder and more brazen in the digital age. Russia has interfered or attempted to interfere in elections from France to the Netherlands, from the Balkans to the Baltics. We've seen Mr. Putin's government use of quote-unquote, "active measures," including support for far-right and far-left parties opposed to historically successful European institutions and post-World War II Western alliances.

For example, Russia has provided support and financial assistance to the far-right party of Marine Le Pen in France in a very blatant and obvious way. Russia has launched cyber attacks against political parties and government institutions in several Western countries. They've also released stolen information in an effort to steer elections in a particular direction, as we saw in the French elections with their release of information about then-candidate Macron.

Germany's parliament has been cyber-attacked with members' e-mails hacked and stolen. Most observers expect this stolen information to be utilized before this fall's national elections in Germany.

As in the United States, Russia aggressively uses trolls and bots to spread fake news and disinformation, with the goal of weakening European institutions and driving a wedge between the United States and Europe. These active measures have been supported by state-controlled Russian media, including RT and Sputnik.

So far, these Russian efforts have not been as successful in Europe as perhaps they were here in the United States. For instance, in France the Macron campaign and the French government were prepared to push back on cyber leaks as they released that information in the 48-hour blackout period. And we've seen companies such as Facebook actually take down a series of fake accounts to help blunt those efforts.

In the Netherlands, earlier this spring officials actually hand-counted paper ballots to ensure that there would be no electronic interference in the vote count. Across Europe, government and media have pushed back against fake news stories and have established such institutions such as the E.U.'s Strategic Communications Division and the NATO Strategic Communications Center of Excellence to educate the public in identifying and correcting Russian propaganda.

Frankly, we have learned a thing or two from our allies in Europe about proactively protecting ourselves against these threats posed by Russia. Months ago, I would have assumed this hearing would have been a good opportunity for the United States to actually import some lessons learned to our European friends. Unfortunately, to date we've not yet as a government in the whole taken to heart many of those lessons.

Unfortunately, as we've heard in testimony before our Committee, our President and his Administration have frankly demonstrated little interest in determining how the Russians did what they did or how we might better protect ourselves going forward. Instead, we've seen the President repeatedly deny that Russia was responsible for U.S. election interference, even in the face of unanimous agreement among our Nation's intelligence agencies.

He's consistently questioned the integrity of our intelligence professionals and he's been all over the map in discussing the United States' commitment to the trans-Atlantic alliances such as NATO.

As several of my colleagues on the Committee have previously noted, in 2016 the Russians targeted Democrats. Who is to say which party will be in the crosshairs next time? The one thing we know is that Vladimir Putin is not a Democrat nor a Republican. His interests are to advance Russia's interests and undermine the United States. In 2016, I believe that Russia got its money's worth in sowing doubt, distrust, and dissension in the heart of the American political process. And my fear is, with that rate of return, that Russia will continue to return to those tactics.

I don't believe anyone believes that Russia will stop and I believe, as a State that has statewide elections in 2017, we have to be alert now. That's why last week when we had DHS before this Committee, we asked them to share, even if they have to share confidentially, the names of the 21 states that were attacked by the Russians in 2016.

I have written and spoken with Secretary Kelly on this matter. As the oversight Committee, I believe we are entitled to that information and we need to work through a process so that State election officials have the security clearances to at least be read in.

And my fear is, as we heard last week, when the top election official from Indiana and the top election official from Wisconsin—both of those states could not acknowledge whether they were part of those 21 states.

And what was also remarkable was we heard from the State of Illinois, which has testified openly that they were attacked on a regular basis, yet they had not been informed until last week that those attacks originated from Russia.

That's why the testimony we hear today is so important to learn lessons from what's happening in Europe and around the world and how on a going-forward basis Western alliances, our Western allies, can stop this very critical 21st century threat.

Thank you, Mr. Chairman. I look forward to the testimony of our witnesses.

Chairman BURR. I thank the Vice Chairman.

At this time, I'd make members aware that we will recognize members by seniority for five minutes.

And I'd also like to make a note to members that when we return from next week's Fourth of July recess, we will immediately consider the nomination of David Glawe, Under Secretary of Intelligence and Analysis at the Department of Homeland Security. If members have additional questions for Mr. Glawe, they need to be in quickly, so that they can be acted on while we're out. I intend—the Vice Chairman and I intend to move that nomination as quickly as we possibly can when we get back.

Again, I thank our witnesses for being here today. I will recognize from my left to my right, and we'll start with you, Ambassador Burns. Welcome.

STATEMENT OF AMBASSADOR NICHOLAS BURNS, PROFESSOR OF DIPLOMACY, HARVARD KENNEDY SCHOOL OF GOVERNMENT

Ambassador BURNS. Mr. Chairman, Mr. Vice Chairman, members of the Committee: Thank you very much for this opportunity to testify. I appreciate very much the bipartisan commitment that your Committee has shown to investigate Russia's interference in the European elections and in our own elections.

There is no doubt about Russia's systematic campaign to undermine our 2016 presidential election, the Montenegrin, Dutch, French and German elections this year, and Russia seeking to diminish the confidence that the citizens of all these countries have in their democracies. In this sense, Russia's actions pose an existential threat to the democratic nations of the West and it requires a swift and serious response by Europeans as well as Americans.

You asked for our recommendations, Mr. Chairman, so I have just three.

First, the United States and Europe need to work much more closely together to identify Russia's cyber and disinformation attacks as they are being launched; and then we need to work together actually to do something about it, to respond in tandem to discredit Russia's actions. You saw the campaign of Emmanuel Macron do that very effectively. You have not seen that in other countries.

We on both sides of the Atlantic should also make it clear to the Russian government that we have our own capabilities that can be injurious to Moscow and that we will use them if Moscow doesn't cease and desist.

With this in mind and with the benefit of hindsight, President Obama in my own view should have been more transparent and specific with the American people during the campaign about the nature of the Russian threat. He should have reacted earlier and much more vigorously.

Now, to be fair to him, this was an extraordinarily difficult choice. It was a new and unexpected threat. President Obama would have likely been accused in the heat of the campaign for intervening in the contest between Secretary Clinton and Donald Trump. And he did make the right call in the end by imposing sanctions on Moscow.

But we in America and Europe have to learn from this experience and try to avoid that in the future.

Second, the U.S. and Europe should adopt stronger sanctions against Russia for its actions to weaken our elections. We learned an important lesson in the Iran nuclear negotiations in the Obama and George W. Bush Administrations: The sanctions were much more effective when the United States and the E.U. aligned them together, specifically the financial sanctions.

I hope the House of Representatives will back and not dilute in this sense the very strong Senate sanctions bill against Moscow that you passed by a 97-to-2 margin two weeks ago. In my view, it would be a grave mistake of President Trump to veto such a bill. And with our long national two-century debate about the separation of powers in mind, I do think that Congress—it's time for the Congress, and not the President, to lead the American response to Russia's cyber attack on the United States.

The President has shown that he's unwilling to act against Russia and that is why the Congressional review provision in your Senate bill makes eminent sense, so that the Administration cannot ease or lift the sanctions on Russia until Putin's attacks on our democratic elections has ceased and until he's met the provisions of the two Minsk agreements on Ukraine and Crimea.

Third, Congress and the President must make resistance to Russian interference in the European elections, as well as ours, an urgent national priority. I served in the government for a long time. I served both parties as a Foreign Service officer. And I find it dismaying and objectionable that President Trump continues to deny the undeniable fact that Russia launched a major cyber attack against the United States, regardless of what party he launched it against.

He's done the same thing in Europe, very systematically. And yet, in response to that President Trump has refused to launch an investigation of his own. He's not made this an issue in our relationship with the Russians. He's taken no steps, at least that I'm aware of, with the Congress and State and local governments to strengthen our voting systems from future Russian hacking of our midterm elections in 2018 and of the next presidential election in 2020. There is no indication he's asked his senior Cabinet officials to develop a plan to protect the United States and to deter the Russians.

And his failure to act—and I'm a former U.S. Ambassador to NATO, I was President George W. Bush's Ambassador—we have a political responsibility in NATO to protect each other, not just from armed conventional attacks, but from cyber attacks as well. That's a clear failure.

I've worked for both parties. It's inconceivable to me that any of President Trump's predecessors would deny the gravity of such an open attack on our democratic system. I don't believe any previous American President would argue that your own hearings in the Senate are a waste of time or, in the words of President Trump, a witch hunt. They're not; you're doing your duty that the people elected you to do.

It is his duty—President Trump's—to be skeptical of Russia. It's his duty to investigate and defend our country against a cyber offensive, because Russia's our most dangerous adversary in the world today; and if he continues to refuse to act, it's a dereliction of the basic duty to defend the country.

And Russia's going to do this again. You heard Director Comey at this Committee say that he felt that Russia would be back maybe against the Republican or Democratic Party. Our elections will be at risk when that happens and the sanctity of our elections will be compromised in the minds of our citizens.

Let me just close by saying that Russia is really testing the leadership and resolve of the West. Americans and Europeans are far stronger in our democratic traditions and our values than the Russians. And with this in mind, we need to be more effective in countering them.

And we can do that by building bipartisan unity in the Congress. And I do want to commend you, Mr. Chairman and Mr. Vice Chairman. You've set a bipartisan tone, which is deeply appreciated. We can do that by encouraging the President to act. We can do that by being very closely aligned with the Europeans to take common action. And I think if we can achieve those three things, we can defeat President Putin and the Russian intelligence services.

Thank you.

[The prepared statement of Ambassador Burns follows:]

HARVARD UNIVERSITY
JOHN F. KENNEDY SCHOOL OF GOVERNMENT
Robert and Renée Belfer Center for Science and International Affairs

R. Nicholas Burns
Roy and Barbara Goodman Family Professor
of Diplomacy and International Relations

79 John F. Kennedy Street
Cambridge, Massachusetts 02138
tel (617) 496-3255

Testimony on Russian Interference in European Elections
Senate Select Committee on Intelligence
Ambassador (ret.) Nicholas Burns
June 28, 2017

Mr. Chairman, Mr. Vice Chairman and members of the Committee, thank you for this opportunity to testify before the Senate Select Committee on Intelligence on Russian government interference in the European elections.

I appreciate and support the bipartisan commitment of this committee to investigate Russia's actions in the 2016 U.S. elections and its similar assault on elections in the Netherlands, France, Germany and other European countries this year and last.

This Russian campaign on both sides of the Atlantic is directed towards one overarching goal—to undermine the democracies of the West, to divide Europe from America, and to weaken both NATO and the European Union. The facts are unassailable—Russia has undertaken a new and aggressive initiative to attack the credibility of what is central and precious in our democracies—our elections. Russia's actions include the publication of outright lies on social media, fake polls, the hacking of the Hillary Clinton and Emmanuel Macron campaigns and the penetration of electoral data bases in at least 21 American states in 2016. This campaign amounts to nothing less than an existential threat to the West.

We know that Russia first practiced this hybrid assault on elections and democratic institutions in the Balkans and Eastern Europe. We know that Russia conducted a systematic campaign to intervene and interfere in the U.S. Presidential election in 2016. We know Russia is currently implementing a similar campaign in Western Europe.

These activities are part of a larger Russian strategy to reduce U.S. power and influence in the world. At the same time, Russian President Vladimir Putin has sought to expand Russia's direct influence over his neighbors. During the last decade, Putin has invaded both Georgia and Ukraine, annexed Crimea, maintained a frozen conflict in Moldova and has consistently harassed our NATO allies, Estonia, Latvia and Lithuania.

Putin is seeking to re-divide Europe south and west of the Russian Federation and to intimidate Russia's neighboring states from the Caucasus region to the Baltic Sea. In the Middle East, his military intervention in Syria in 2015 was designed, in part, to diminish U.S. power, maneuverability and credibility in the Levant. These are among the many reasons that Russia is our most dangerous adversary in the world today.

HARVARD UNIVERSITY
JOHN F. KENNEDY SCHOOL OF GOVERNMENT
Robert and Renée Belfer Center for Science and International Affairs

R. Nicholas Burns
Roy and Barbara Goodman Family Professor
of Diplomacy and International Relations

79 John F. Kennedy Street
Cambridge, Massachusetts 02138
tel (617) 496-3255

Since the end of the Cold War, American policy towards Russia has been built on a bipartisan foundation. I served Presidents of both parties as an advisor on Russian affairs at the National Security Council and at the State Department. In both Republican and Democratic Administrations, our Presidents from George H.W. Bush to Barack Obama have tried to work with Russia where that was possible, most recently in Afghanistan, on the Iran Nuclear issue and on North Korea.

All of these Presidents resolved, however, to defend the NATO alliance against Russian aggression, to support the independence and territorial integrity of Ukraine and Georgia and to oppose Russian actions in the Balkans to undercut established governments in that region. The major U.S. and European priority for two decades now has been to advance our democracies, their leading role in global affairs and to protect the integrity of our democratic societies at home.

U.S. relations with Moscow are now at their lowest point since before Mikhail Gorbachev came to power in the Soviet era more than thirty years ago. There is no trust between Washington and Moscow. We have major strategic disagreements concerning the future of Europe and the Middle East. But, Russia's recent actions to diminish confidence in the integrity of our elections are a grave new threat. And they are potentially harmful to our democratic way of life.

We have learned more just in the last few weeks about how Russia has conducted these operations against our democracies. A recent report by the Atlantic Council (where I am a board member) detailed concerns in Europe that Russian operatives are employing "social bots", untruthful and fake news stories and disinformation to confuse the public debate before Germany's elections in September. That same Council report by its Digital Forensics Lab reminded its readers that the Russian government controls an effective and far-reaching global media platform comprising RT, Sputnik, NewsFront and other services. These Moscow-controlled news agencies are actively spreading false information in Germany about the parties, candidates and issues at the heart of the campaign. What is happening in Germany today happened to us last summer and autumn.

The Trump Administration, the Congress and our European allies need to meet this threat with determination, speed and effectiveness. With that in mind, I have five recommendations to make to the committee this morning.

First, and most importantly, the President and the Congress must make defeating Russia's ambitions a vital national priority. I have been impressed by the degree of bipartisanship by many members of the Congress in both parties and in both houses on this issue.

It has been nothing short of dismaying, however, that President Trump continues to deny the undeniable fact that Russian interfered in our elections in the U.S. and is doing so now in Europe.

Nicholas_Burns@hks.harvard.edu

HARVARD UNIVERSITY
JOHN F. KENNEDY SCHOOL OF GOVERNMENT
Robert and Renée Belfer Center for Science and International Affairs

R. Nicholas Burns
Roy and Barbara Goodman Family Professor
of Diplomacy and International Relations

79 John F. Kennedy Street
Cambridge, Massachusetts 02138
tel (617) 496-3255

He has refused to launch an investigation of his own. He has not made this a priority in his conversations with Russian officials. He has taken no known steps to work with the Congress and with state and local governments to prevent such interference in our 2018 mid-term elections or in the 2020 elections beyond. Senior members of his Administration have admitted that he has never asked for their own views on this problem. And he has not given your committee's bipartisan effort to investigate and to devise countermeasures the support it clearly deserves.

Based on my service in Republican and Democratic Administrations dating back to the Presidency of Jimmy Carter, I cannot imagine any of President Trump's predecessors denying that such a problem existed. None of them would have argued, as he has publicly, that these hearings and your work are a waste of time and a problem manufactured by his political opponents. All of our previous Presidents would have understood that it was their responsibility to investigate, to be skeptical of Russian intentions and to exercise their primary duty to defend our country and our allies from Russian cyber and covert aggression.

We have heard from Secretary Tillerson and Secretary Mattis strong condemnation of Russia's actions. Our intelligence agencies are united in opposition to Moscow. The American public, based on recent polls, is also very concerned.

What we need most of all to counter Russia is for President Trump to take action. We need him to defend the United States against our most aggressive and capable adversary.

Second, the U.S. and Europe must work together to maintain our current sanctions against Russia and to reinforce them where necessary. As we learned with Iran on the nuclear issue in both the Obama and George W. Bush Administrations, sanctions are infinitely more powerful and persuasive when we combine our efforts across the Atlantic.

The Senate's recent vote by a 97-2 margin to pass a tough sanctions bill against Russian interference in our election and for its actions in Ukraine was far-sighted and right. The Senate and House must now reach an agreement on a final bill that will have a major impact on Moscow's calculations. I hope the House of Representatives will not dilute the Senate bill as our response to Russia must be unmistakably clear and powerful. And I certainly hope President Trump will not veto such a measure by arguing that he needs the flexibility to conduct relations with Russia. A hostile foreign power has intervened to sway our elections. There can be only one response—swift and harsh sanctions by the U.S. in return.

The Trump Administration should consider measures of its own to send a stiff message to Moscow. The Administration should maintain all of President Obama's sanctions on the Russian government, including to continue to deny Russian embassy officials access to their facilities in New York and

HARVARD UNIVERSITY
JOHN F. KENNEDY SCHOOL OF GOVERNMENT
Robert and Renée Belfer Center for Science and International Affairs

R. Nicholas Burns
Roy and Barbara Goodman Family Professor
of Diplomacy and International Relations

79 John F. Kennedy Street
Cambridge, Massachusetts 02138
tel (617) 496-3255

Maryland that the U.S. wisely closed in December. This is not the time to extend olive branches to the Russian government.

As someone whose government service has been solely in the Executive Branch, I have always favored protecting the authority and power of the President to act decisively on national security issues. Given President Trump's weak and ill-advised views toward Russia, however, it is prudent for the Senate and House to insist on a process of Congressional review of the Russia sanctions so that President Trump cannot relax them before Putin has met all the conditions in the Minsk agreements and reversed the annexation of Crimea.

This is a time in our long national debate over the separation of powers that Congress must provide the tough-minded strategic leadership for our country on Russia given the President's unwillingness and inability to do so.

The U.S., Canadian and European sanctions on Russia will be even more effective if they are enforced vigorously, if violators are punished and if we fill in some of the loopholes that give European firms license to continue investments in the Russian economy when American companies cannot do so.

Third, NATO and the EU should work more closely together to strengthen our democracies in order to resist Russia's campaign to weaken us. Specifically, we should establish joint working groups of our intelligence agencies and foreign ministries to share information in real time on Russia's campaign of disruption in our elections. We should also respond quickly with efforts of our own to discredit Russian propaganda on social media and in more established print, radio and television networks. The campaign of French President Emmanuel Macron was particularly effective in recognizing Russia's disinformation campaign and then reacting quickly and effectively to expose it publicly. We in America can learn from France and other European countries on how best to counter Russia's active measures against us.

We must also work with Canada and Europe to strengthen our local and state electoral arrangements— the sanctity of voting rolls and the procedures for tabulating votes-- to harden our systems and to make them significantly more resistant to hacking and manipulation by Russian agents.

And there must be a price for Putin to pay if he continues this assault on democracy. With the benefit of hindsight, the Obama Administration should have reacted more quickly and vigorously last summer and autumn to respond to the Russian hacking of the Democratic National Committee and its effort to harm Secretary Hillary Clinton's campaign. It should have been much more transparent with the American public about what it knew and the threat it clearly posed to the election. But, at least President Obama's administration eventually took action to sanction Russian officials for the part they played in this aggression. The same cannot be said for President Trump and his administration.

Nicholas_Burns@hks.harvard.edu

HARVARD UNIVERSITY
JOHN F. KENNEDY SCHOOL OF GOVERNMENT
Robert and Renée Belfer Center for Science and International Affairs

R. Nicholas Burns
Roy and Barbara Goodman Family Professor
of Diplomacy and International Relations

79 John F. Kennedy Street
Cambridge, Massachusetts 02138
tel (617) 496-3255

We need to learn everything possible about how Russia penetrated our campaign websites and electoral processes as there is every indication it will continue its actions against us. The United States and Europe have the capability to respond in ways that will be injurious to the Kremlin. If its interference in our elections does not stop, the U.S. should act in concert with Europe to remind Russian leaders of this central fact.

Fourth, another important way to resist and undermine Russia is to strengthen the security of our NATO allies and our other friends in Eastern Europe. President Obama and the Congress already began this effort by agreeing to the deployment of NATO battalions to Poland, Estonia, Latvia and Lithuania. This sent a strong signal to Russia that we will defend those NATO allies who live in Russia's shadow. The U.S. and its allies should make these deployments permanent to demonstrate our strong resolve.

The Congress has also funded during the last two years a substantial rebuilding of the U.S. military's armored strength in Europe. That effort should continue. In addition to these steps, the U.S. should now consider transferring lethal defensive arms to Ukraine so that it can defend itself from outright Russian theft of part of its territory. All of these steps will help us to contain Russian power in Eastern Europe until the Putin generation passes from power in the next decade or so.

Fifth and finally, resistance to Russia must be seen by all of us as a fundamental test of American leadership in the Transatlantic world. We in the West are stronger than Russia. Much of that strength rests not just on our arms but on our values and democratic traditions.

We are in a major contest with Russia over the future of Europe. Many of us thought the struggle for a democratic, peaceful and united Europe had been won a quarter century ago with the fall of communism in the Warsaw Pact countries and the fall of the Soviet Union itself. But Moscow is now contesting that historical achievement. It is seeking to weaken the western democracies and to intimidate its neighbors.

More than anything else, we need to be unified in the West to prevail. That is why it is vital for President Trump to return to an open embrace of our European allies in his trip to Europe next week. His persistent criticism of NATO and his outright ambivalence about the European Union have harmed the credibility of the United States in Europe. They have cast doubt on our seven decades-long strategy to build peace and security in Europe and to stand by our Article V commitment to NATO.

Since World War Two, the American President has been the leader of the West. By denying that Russian actions are a challenge for the future of the western democracies, President Trump has sadly abdicated that role. We can only hope that he will eventually reconsider and provide more powerful leadership in the tradition of all our modern Presidents of both parties from Harry S Truman and Dwight D. Eisenhower to George W. Bush and Barack Obama.

Nicholas_Burns@hks.harvard.edu

HARVARD UNIVERSITY
JOHN F. KENNEDY SCHOOL OF GOVERNMENT

Robert and Renée Belfer Center for Science and International Affairs

R. Nicholas Burns
Roy and Barbara Goodman Family Professor
of Diplomacy and International Relations

79 John F. Kennedy Street
Cambridge, Massachusetts 02138
tel (617) 496-3255

In order to meet the challenge of Russia's assault on our democracies, we need bipartisan unity in the Congress, Presidential leadership in the White House and a concerted effort with our European allies to defend our democracies currently under assault. If we can secure these three things, we can prevail in defeating this pernicious threat from Moscow.

Nicholas_Burns@hks.harvard.edu

Chairman BURR. Thank you, Ambassador, and thank you for your service for a long time to this country.

Ambassador Garcevic.

STATEMENT OF AMBASSADOR VESKO GARCEVIC, PROFESSOR OF DIPLOMACY, PARDEE SCHOOL OF GLOBAL STUDIES, BOSTON UNIVERSITY

Ambassador GARCEVIC. Thank you, Mr. Chairman Burr, Mr. Vice Chairman Warner, distinguished members of the Committee. Thank you very much for giving me the opportunity to speak on Russia's interference in Montenegro's home affairs.

On October 16, 2016, Montenegro held its parliamentary elections. The plotters, disguised in police uniforms, were preparing to storm the Montenegrin Parliament and provoke a turmoil by shooting at citizens waiting for the election results. In the final stage, the plotters intended to detain or assassinate the Prime Minister. Acting on a tip from an informant, Montenegrin police were able to arrest most of the plot suspects.

In the indictment filed recently, 14 people were charged, including two opposition politicians and two Russian agents, Vladimir Popov and Eduard Shirokov, members of the Russian Military Intelligence Service who are identified as the ringleaders of the operation.

How do we know that? For example, Shirokov, alias Sismakov, was posted as the assistant military attache at the Russian embassy in Warsaw until Poland declared him persona non grata for espionage. The whereabouts of Shirokov and Popov are unknown, while Russian authorities never replied or provided information about the suspects.

The coup plot is the culmination of more than 18 months long-synchronized actions against Montenegro, which include an aggressive media campaign, coupled with open support to pro-Russian political parties in Montenegro.

While Russia has been consistent in making threatening gestures over Montenegro's NATO bid, they never—they have never specified what their intentions are. But for example, when Montenegro joined NATO recently, at the beginning of June, Moscow commented that in response to Montenegro's anti-Russian hysteria and hostile policy, Russia reserves the right to take reciprocal measures.

There are more than 100 Moscow-backed organizations and media outlets at this moment in the region. In an anti-Montenegro media campaign, the NATO invitation is described as a move to challenge Moscow. The Montenegrin government is labeled as treacherous and corrupted, a pawn in the hands of the U.S. and NATO; and Russia, stronger than ever, is the only state standing in their way.

The Orthodox Church too is utilized to promote the values of Orthodox Christianity and present them as fundamentally different, that fundamentally contradicts the Western world. The Russian government fully backs democratic fronts and an anti-NATO political coalition dominated by Serbian Nationalist Party, known for their pro-Russian affiliation. The primary goal of the front and its supporters in Russia was to get the Montenegrin opposition united around its political platform and prevent the formation of a new pro-NATO government in Montenegro.

Moscow has made no progress in Montenegro and it has seemingly lost a possibility of having a strategically significant outlet on the Adriatic coast. But Moscow will continue exploiting loopholes that exist in most of the Balkan states: democratic incapacity, corruption, ethnic tensions, countries' economic and military needs, and growing feelings of marginalization of those countries on their part to the E.U. and NATO.

The rule of law, independent institutions, and efficient law enforcement agencies are the precondition for stability and effective protection from Russia's influence. The best way to restrain Russian interference is a proactive approach from the U.S. and the E.U. side and energetic support for democratic reforms in the Balkan states. The door of NATO and the E.U. must remain open for states wishing to join those organizations. And further American retreat may have a lasting adverse implication for Balkan and European security.

Thank you, Mr. Chairman, and I'm looking forward for your questions.

[The prepared statement of Ambassador Garcevic follows:]

THE US SENATE SELECT COMMITTEE ON INTELLIGENCE: RUSSIAN INTERFIRENCE IN EUROPEAN ELECTIONS

Russia and Montenegro

Testimony of Ambassador Vesko Garčević
Professor of the Practice of International Relations
The Frederick Pardee School of Global Studies
Boston University
June 28, 2017, Washington DC

Dear Mr. Chairman Burr, Dear Vice Chairman Warner, Distinguished Members of the Senate Committee on Intelligence. Thank you very much for giving me the opportunity to speak to you today on continuous Russia's interference in Montenegro's home affairs over the past few years.

Introduction

For years, the Balkans has slipped out of the attention of the EU and the US. Not being fully integrated into the European and Euro-Atlantic structures, it has become an ideal target for Russia that found its way to influence regional Governments and sway them to more favorable position for Moscow. Russian politicians, MPs, representatives of various Russian "institutes" and groups are frequently visiting the Region. Semi-official Russian cultural and religious organizations have been flourishing in the recent past. They are established to provide necessary political and financial support to Reginal political parties, leaders, intellectuals, media outlets with a solid Russian connection.

In the Western Balkans[1], Russia has a plenty of soft power means at its disposal. Cultural closeness, historic ties, identical religious roots make Russia and the Russian people close to ordinary citizens in the Balkans, which Russia smartly utilizes to expand its political and economic influence.

Montenegro has a particularly interesting position in Moscow's eyes. Its geographical location makes this country far more relevant in given European security and political context than one may conclude judging its size.

Why is it so important?

---

[1] The institutions of the EU have defined the "Western Balkans" as the south-east European area that includes countries that are not members of the EU: Croatia (now an EU member), Serbia, Bosnia and Herzegovina, Montenegro, Kosovo, Macedonia and Albania

In September 2013, the Russian Federation made what then-Russian ambassador in Montenegro, Andrey Nesterenko, described as "a request" to "discuss the terms of allowing Russian warships temporary moorage at the ports in Montenegro for refueling, maintenance and other necessities." Moscow's request was prompted by the war in Syria and the uncertain future of the Russian naval facility in the Syrian port city of Tartus. Montenegro rejected the request in December of that year. The importance of such facilities in the Mediterranean was demonstrated in October 2016 when the Russian carrier, the Admiral Kuznetsov, and its battle group were denied refueling in European ports on their way to support the Russian military effort in Syria.

That's why Moscow looks at Montenegro's decision to join NATO with displeasure. If Montenegro joins NATO, it would give the alliance control of every northern port in the Mediterranean.

The naval base case has brought Moscow to conclusion that only a change of the current Government in Montenegro may enable Russia to make gains in the small Balkans state and secure its strategic interests in this part of the Adriatic Sea. Being in the middle of the demanding process of the democratic transition marked by challenges such as corruption or weak state institutions and getting split over the issue of NATO membership, Montenegro provided an opportunity for a Moscow's stronger involvement and murky political games.

The coup plot is just a tip of the iceberg, the culmination of more than 18-months long synchronized actions, which includes an aggressive media campaign coupled with the open political and financial support to pro-Russian political parties in Montenegro with an obvious aim – to reverse a pro-western course of the state and prevent it from joining NATO.

Russian Media Campaign in Montenegro

In the Region, Russia has established numerous Moscow based media offices in order to bolster its influence in both Montenegro and the rest of the Balkans. As it appeared to be virtually impossible in Montenegro because the Government of Montenegro can withdraw its licenses at any moment, media outlets are based in neighboring Serbia and from there they have an almost unimpeded access to Montenegro. They all broadcast or print their information in the Serbian language. The Region witnessed an outburst of Russian media in the Serbian language: Sputnik, South Front, Novaya Russia. There are more than 100 Moscow-backed organizations and media outlets active in Serbia in this moment. Sputnik is, by far, the most protuberant media outlet profoundly engaged in the ongoing media war and the anti-Western campaign in the Region.

Portraying Montenegro, Russian media have developed a twofold approach with a set of messages for international public and another for Montenegrin citizens. The campaign had been particularly intensive a few months before Montenegro got an invitation to join NATO on December 2, 2015, and several weeks before and during the Parliamentary elections held in October 16, 2016.

For the international public, Montenegro is depicting as a highly corrupted, politically unstable and problems-burdened state lagging behind all its neighbors, particularly Serbia. The Montenegrin leadership is portrayed as one that doesn't respect international norms and has been involved in numerous criminal activities and, hence, it is to be held responsible and prosecuted. The NATO decision to invite Montenegro to join the Alliance is depicted as an example of "double standards" and a move motivated exclusively by Western interests to challenge Moscow and show disrespect for its international position.

In messages for Montenegro's public, the Montenegrin Government is described as treacherous, corrupted and bribed, a pawn in hands of the US and NATO, not being worthy of support.

Russian media have been exceptionally supportive to extreme right Serb nationalist political groups in Montenegro. Russian arguments are presented to the Montenegrin public through social networks or through web portals of political actors, groups/NGOs that oppose NATO membership of Montenegro. On their side, Russia is depicted as an invincible, stronger than ever power, the guardian of the Orthodox Christianity and an undisputed friend of all the Orthodox peoples. Contrary, NATO is portrayed as a US-led war-bringing organization that wants to control the world and Russia is the only state standing in its way.

In order to penetrate Montenegrin society Russia also utilizes the Orthodox Church for its goals. The Church plays an important social and political role among the orthodox population. It is used to promote "the values of Eastern Christianity" and present them as something which fundamentally contradicts the Western world, i.e. both the EU and NATO. Priests from the Church have been actively engaged in an anti-Western propaganda invented to comfort Russian sentiments. Their statements and accusations are broadly broadcasted by local and Russian media.

An Open Support for anti-NATO and Pro-Russia Protests

Moscow didn't hide that it would like to see the Montenegrin Government replaced by those who could turn the country toward Russia. Democratic front, an anti-NATO political coalition dominated by Serbian nationalist parties[2] known for their pro-Russian affiliation, almost dying on the margin of the Montenegrin political spectrum, was resurrected by the Russian hand to become the biggest opposition formation in the Montenegrin Parliament winning 21 percent of votes at the last Parliamentary elections held in October 2016 or 18 seats out of 81 seats in the Montenegrin Parliament. Their ideas are promoted by pro-Russia's web portals: inf4s (http://www.in4s.net), the portal of the NGO NO to War, NO to NATO (http://www.neunato.net/) and the web site of the Montenegrin Movement for Neutrality (http://mnmne.org/). In some cases, Montenegrin NGO leaders and political activists are on payroll lists of Russian institutions in Serbia. One of the leaders of the anti-NATO campaign in Montenegro, Marko Milacic, was long a correspondent of Sputnik in Montenegro.

A few months before the NATO Ministerial in December 2015, when had become apparent that Montenegro would get NATO invitation, hardcore opponents of NATO, summoned around Democratic Front and backed by Serbian Orthodox Church, with an overt support of Moscow decided to stage "democratic protests" against the Government with an aim to spark the outburst of popular unrests all over the country, "liberate the Parliament" and overturn the Montenegrin leadership. At the beginning of the street protests, organizers were chanting slogans against the corrupted Government and alleged electoral frauds. How protests continued, from slogans, political speeches, anti-NATO and pro-Russian rhetoric of protest leaders, it had become obvious that those behind a "people's awakening" had the only one agenda in their mind: how to prevent Montenegro from becoming the next member of NATO and how to bring Montenegro back to the Russian hug.

Russia's involvement in Montenegro is unique compared to the Maiden protests in Ukraine for two reasons: 1) The Russian government was openly supporting the protestors who wanted to overthrow a democratically elected Government which was not the case in Ukraine. In its reaction from October 17, 2015, the Russian Ministry of Foreign Affairs deplored the events in Montenegro emphasizing "it is impossible to overlook the fact that, contrary to the assurances that Western states are giving Montenegrin leaders, the involvement of this country in the process of Euro-Atlantic integration does not lead to its consolidation and prosperity. On the contrary, we are witnessing the political and ideological polarization of society and the escalation of socioeconomic problems. One gets the impression that plans for the expedite promotion of Montenegro into NATO simultaneously contemplate the suppression of

---

[2] Democratic Front is composed of the New Serbian Democracy (NOVA), Movement for Changes (PzP), Democratic People's Party (DNP), Workers' Party (RP), Democratic Party of Unity (DSJ), Yugoslav Communist Party of Montenegro (JKP), Democratic Serb Party (DSS), Resistance to Hopelessness (OB), Party of United Pensioners and the Disabled (PUPI) and Serb Radical Party (SRS).

alternative approaches." 2) Russia politically endorsed Democratic Front and actors affiliated to it.

Russian Federation and Democratic Front

Leaders of Democratic Front are frequent visitors to Moscow. Almost every month leaders of the Front pay visits to either Russian state institutions or Russian institutes for foreign relations. Their last visits took place just few weeks ago. Delegations of Democratic Front are regularly met by high-ranking Russian officials who are recognized for their connections with the war in Ukraine, including Vice President Dmitry Rogozin, Speaker and Deputy Speaker of Duma Sergey Naryshkin and Sergei Zheleznyak, former Director of the Russian Institute for Strategic Studies Leonid Resetnikov and so on. During those visits, in accordance with public statements, leaders of Democratic Front discussed a new course of action after having been defeated at the Parliamentary elections in Montenegro.

During one of those visits, the idea of neutral Montenegro, the "Balkans Switzerland" was born. This notion was coined by Sergei Zheleznyak, a prominent member of Putin's party and former deputy Speaker of the Russian Parliament. Zheleznyak is on the US black list of Russians who supported the Crimean annexation and the one who co-authored a law which would force internationally funded non-profit organizations to register as "foreign agents". He advised Montenegrin political cronies to promote the neutrality as a counter-argument against the membership to NATO. Russian interlocutors promised an unwavering support to Democratic Front so as to facilitate their triumph in the upcoming Parliamentary Elections in Montenegro. Leaders of Democratic Front, from their side, gave a firm word that they would reverse Montenegro's support of the EU sanctions against Russia. They underlined the commitment to revoke the Montenegrin Euro-Atlantic integration.

Russia's officials about Montenegro's membership in NATO

Russian officials and Ministry of Foreign Affairs have made several indicative statements about Montenegro since it has been invited to join NATO. A couple of them are particularly symptomatic and suggestive and can be perceived, at least, as stirring for what will be happening during the electoral campaign in Montenegro, including the coup attempt. While Russia has been consistent with making threatening gestures over Montenegro's NATO integration, they have also never specified what they were/are planning to do.

When NATO allies, on December 2, 2015, invited Montenegro to join the Alliance, President Vladimir Putin's spokesman Dmitry Peskov stressed that Russia has repeatedly warned that "the continuing expansion of NATO and the military infrastructure of NATO to the east cannot fail to lead to actions in response from the east -- that is, from Russia." As he explained the action would be aimed "to provide for [Russia's] security interests and support parity" between Moscow and the Alliance.

The Russian Ministry of Foreign Affairs describes the decision "to launch NATO accession talks with Montenegro as an openly confrontationist move which is fraught with additional destabilizing consequences for the system of Euro-Atlantic security" and concludes that "this new round of the alliance's expansion directly affects the interests of the Russian Federation and forces us to respond accordingly."

In a response to the signing of the Protocol of Accession of Montenegro to NATO, on May 19, 2016, the Russian Ministry accused NATO for "attempts to change the military and political landscape in Europe, in particular, in the context of its outspoken policy of deterrence towards Russia" and made it clear that this, "will inevitably affect Russia's interests and force it to respond proportionately," According to the statement, "dragging Montenegro into NATO won't be left without Russia's reaction". This is followed by similar accusations of other Russian officials including minister of foreign affairs Sergej Lavrov and his deputy Aleksej Miskov.

It goes without saying that above mentioned arguments were reverberated by leaders of Democratic Front during the election campaign.

Parliamentary Elections in Montenegro and A Coup Plot

Democratic Front was running an intensive, aggressive and very costly political campaign in Montenegro throughout 2016. Its broad mobilizing action was backed by the Serbian Orthodox Church, numerous NGOs both in Montenegro and Serbia, intellectuals renowned for their pro-Russian opinions and some political parties from the region with the similar ideology. This network served and still serves as an extended and agile component of Democratic Front. In spite of an exceptionally expensive campaign, Front leaders have never provided a comprehensive information on financial sources for their campaign.

The primary goal of Democratic Front and their supporters in Russia was to get the Montenegrin opposition united around the Democratic Front's platform for action and prevent the strongest party in Montenegro, Democratic Party of Socialist, from gaining majority in the Parliament that would enable the formation of a new pro-NATO Government.

The Coup Plot

On October 16, 2016, Montenegro held its parliamentary elections. The plotters disguised in police uniforms were preparing to storm the Montenegrin Parliament and provoke a turmoil by shooting at citizens waiting for the election results. Following the incident, they would declare that the party of their choice (Democratic Front) had won the elections. In the final stage of the action, the plotters intended to unlawfully detain or assassinate the Prime Minister of Montenegro. Acting on a tip from an informant, Montenegrin police were able to abrupt the violence and arrest most of the plot suspects, including the former commander of the Serbian Gendarmerie, Bratislav Dikic. The Prosecutors Office has interrogated more than 20 suspects, 14 of them were taken into custody, while others were released.

Montenegrin state authorities (the Supreme State Prosecutor and the Special Prosecutor for Organized Crime and Corruption) publicly presented some pieces of evidence to prove their claim and justify their action against the plot suspects. This included intercepted phone conversations between Bratislav Dikic and Aleksandar Sindjelic, a supposed founder of the pro-Russian organization in Serbia "The Serbian Wolves". According to Krym.Realii, Sindjelic has fought in the Eastern Ukraine on the side of the Russian-backed forces.

Sindjelic and Dikic accepted to cooperate with the Prosecutor Office.They provided information about key links between suspected terrorists, nationalist Russian structures and, possibly, some political subjects in Montenegro. They confirmed that the action was carefully prepared both in Serbia and Montenegro. Dikic and the core group of plotters arrived in Montenegro a few days before the general elections with the aim to organize two groups of plotters and make things ready for their action during the election day. Sindjelic confessed his key role in "recruiting other members of the organization, transferring money between the organizers and members of the group, providing weapons, phones, buying police equipment, uniforms, shields, batons, body armours, tear gas, gas masks and other equipment that would be used by the group members during the attack on the Parliament." According to the police sources, Sindjelic received €200,000 from the Russians and distributed the money to members of the criminal group. Dikic, for example, received €15,000.

Following statements of Montenegrin authorities, the Serbia's Prime Minister, in his press announcement, revealed the information of Serbia's Intelligence agancy that there had been a preparation of "illegal activities" in Serbia to be carried out on Montenegrin territory. He confirmed that the Serbian police identified and arrested several persons who closely monitored and stalked Prime Minister of Montenegro, M. Djukanovic, and informed another group, including "foreign elements", about that. He added that there were numerous proofs for his claims, including photographs, videos, intercepted phone conversations, uniforms, confiscated money (€120,000 in cash) as well as legal confessions of some suspects involved in the plot. Russian daily Kommersant wrote that these groups used encrypted telephones, two of which were discovered in Serbia and in Montenegro, and the third one, "located in Russia", was out of reach.

Nemanja Ristic, the person from Serbia suspected of being one of the key plotters is still at large. He has been revealed by Serbian media as photographed standing near Russian foreign minister Sergey Lavrov. The mentioned photo had been made on December 12 2016, during Lavrov's visit to Belgrade while meeting with Serbian far-right grouping members. Among them, there was Nemanja Ristic. The Serbian police keeps him under police surveliance, but they didn't yet deport him to Montenegro despite the Interpol red notice issued by the request of Montenegrin jurisdictions.

In the 135 pages indictment filed recently, the Montenegro's chief prosecutor charges 14 people, including two Montenegrin oposition politicians and two Russian agents, Vladimir Popov and Eduard Shirokov, members of the Russian Military Intelligence Service – GRU, who are identified as the ringleaders of the operation. The GRU is the same organization sanctioned by the US for hacking the Democratic National Committee offices. Shirokov, alias Shishmakov, was posted as the assistant military attaché at the Russian Embassy in Poland until 2014 when Poland declared him persona non-grata for espionage. Shirokov, got a new identity and false Russian documents in August last year, two months before the elections in Montenegro. Popov and Shirokov were then dispatched to Montenegro's next door neighbor Serbia from where they coordinated coup preparations. They were expelled from Serbia to Russia several weeks after the coup. The whereabouts of Shirokov and Popov are unknown while Russian state authorities have never replied to Montenegro's requests to provide information about the suspects.

The Coup: The Balkans Cossacks Army

It should be noted that all conspirators arrested in actions of the Montenegro's and Serbia's police enjoy the reputation of being supporters of pro-Russian nationalist extremist groups and Russian separatists in the Eastern Ukraine. One of those Russian extremist organizations has a special place in this case as many of the plotters have been either closely connected to it or they have been members of it. It is the so-called Balkans Cossacks Army, an offspring of the Russian Cossacks Army, a semi-military nationalistic, pan-Slav association linked to the Russian army and secret services. As the investigation indicates, the Balkans Cossacks Army is likely used to reach out people willing to take part in the plot, motivate and organize them and prepare them for the execution of the plan.

The Balkans Cossack Army was formed in Kotor, Montenegro on September 11, 2016 (the date, September 11, was chosen on purpose) with the support of Night Wolves, the Russian biker organization close to Vladimir Putin. The Night Wolves are banned from entering the United States, Poland, Germany, and Canada.[3] The Cossacks are known for their efforts to "unite the orthodox world and advance the Russian world". Cossack "general" Viktor Vladimirovich Zaplatin has been unanimously elected supreme ataman (commander) of the Balkan Cossack Army. Zaplatin has been living in Serbia for 16 years and enjoys reputation of one who has good connections with Russian officials. He fought in Bosnia in 1992-93, as well as in conflicts in the Georgian regions of Abkhazia and South Ossetia, in the Azerbaijani region of Nagorno-Karabakh, and in the Moldovan region of Transnistria. Zaplatin is described in the pro-Russian press in Serbia as "the official representative of the Union of Volunteers, which is directly associated with Vladimir Putin." Priests of the Serbian Orthodox Church were present at the event to bless the formation of the Balkans Cossack Army.

The key coup plotters from Serbia are closely tied with the Balkans Cossack Army whereas Sindjelic publicly admitted his connection with the Night Wolves. Representatives of the Balkans Cossack Army visited Moscow from October 11 through October 16.

The building of paramilitary and extremist forces to be used abroad as proxies is an age-old tactic. The Russian newspaper *Novaya Gazeta* in an article published at the beginning of November 2016 highlighted how Cossacks and Serbian volunteers, who fought in the Eastern Ukraine, are used by Russian secret services to carry out sensitive operations in the Balkans.

---

[3] https://www.treasury.gov/press-center/press-releases/Pages/jl9729.aspx

The Coup: Russian official reactions

Moscow officially denied any involvement in the Montenegrin October's events. After the Montenegrin Government was formed, Russian Foreign Ministry issued statement urging Montenegro to chart a "balanced course in foreign policy", which is yet another diplomatic warning that Russia will defend its "sphere of interest" in the Balkans. The Montenegrin government and especially former Prime Minister Djukanovic were harshly criticized by Russian Minister of Foreign Affairs Sergei Lavrov. In December 2016, he stated that EU is pressuring Serbia to act like "Montenegro, who broke all its promises and betrayed Russia".

The same day, on June 5, when Montenegro formally joined NATO, the Russian Foreign Ministry commented that in response to Montenegro's "anti-Russian hysteria" and "hostile policy," Russia "reserves the right to take reciprocal measures." This was yet another public warning from Russia's side though they didn't explicitly mention what kind of counter-measures Moscow is considering to take against Montenegro.

In spite of the Russian firm denial of any connection with the plot, a few Russian moves may denote the Moscow's involvement in the case:

1. Sergei Petrushev, the former head of the Federal Security Service of the Russian Federation and the current Head of Russian Security Council arrived in Serbia a few days after the coup. His visit coincided with reported expulsions of several Russian citizens from Serbia, which seemingly included Popov and Shirokov. The deportation seemed to have happened after the Petrushev intervention.

2. On November 4, 2016 President of Russian Federation, Vladimir Putin released retired general Leonid Reshetnikov from his duties as Director of the Russian Institute for Strategic Studies (RISS), effective January 4, 2017, and appointed Mikhail Fradkov, the former Prime Minister of Russia and the head of Russia's Foreign Intelligence Service from 6 October 2007 to 5 October 2016, as a new Director. This decision not only illustrates the profile of the "Institute", but also came soon after Petrushev's visit to Belgrade.

Reshetnikov is known for his extreme anti-NATO and anti-American position. He is seen to be heavily engaged in the region and attempts to reverse Montenegrin NATO integration. Being close to nationalist, pan-Slavic Russian groups and organizations linked to separatists in Ukraine and involved in the war in this country, he welcomed the establishment of the Balkans Cossack Army as "another uniting factor of Orthodox Slovenian nations in the Balkans". The dismissal of Reshetnikov is likely a result of Petrushev's talks in Belgrade and consultations with President Putin.

Cyber attacks

During election campaign and voting day, several Montenegrin on-line media were subjected to cyber-attacks, which resulted in temporary disruptions of their services. The online news portals CaffeDelMontenegro (one of the most popular online portals in Montenegro) and "Antena M", which are recognized for their support to NATO membership of Montenegro, were attacked several times. Moreover, web pages of the Government of Montenegro, Democratic Party of Socialists and Center for Democratic Transition (one of NGOs observing the elections, known for its support to NATO) were also attacked. It has been estimated by Montenegrin authorities that these cyber-attacks were the strongest ever encountered by Montenegro's information system. The cyber-attacks have not been stopped ever since, official sites, and networks, as well as online media, have been methodically subjected to cyber-attacks up until the present day.

Conclusion:

Montenegro appeared to be a failed case for Russia, one of only a few cases that Moscow has lately lost in its ongoing zero-sum style competition with the West. Despite its efforts and money, Moscow has made no measurable progress in getting Montenegro on its side, and it has seemingly lost a possibility of having a strategically significant outlet on the Adriatic Sea.

1. *NATO open door policy must remain as vibrant as before*:

Russia should not have a veto right on NATO expansion, but it proved to have the capacity to threaten, influence and subvert the process as it was the case with Georgia. It's why Montenegro matters more than it looks at the first sight. The Montenegrin case confirms, once again, what Russia is capable of doing to make its interests come through. The Balkans is one of several European playgrounds between Moscow on one side and the US and the EU on the other. Russia's long-term strategy is to drag its rivals' involvement down to a level that would make countries of the region subjects to Moscow's interference. This part of Europe has long been low on the list of American priorities and any further American retreat may have lasting adverse implications for this region particularly and the European security in general, which may eventually be detrimental to America's enduring interests in Europe.

2. *To restraint Russia's influence a continuous pro-active approach is needed from the US and the EU side in countries wishing to join NATO and the EU. Democratic transition in aspiring countries should be reinforced: the rule of law, fight against corruption and strengthening of institutions are the precondition for stability and an effective protection from Russia's influence*

The Russian Federation will continue to exploit loopholes that exist in most of the Balkans states: democratic incapacity, corruption, ethnic tensions, countries' economic and/or military needs, and growing feelings of disenfranchisement of those countries "on the path" to EU and NATO membership. The goal of Russia is not so much to gain partners from which it can benefit economically or militarily (in the sense of physical support). Rather, Russia's intends to keep NATO and the EU out of the Balkans to the fullest extent possible, whether by filling gaps (e.g. economic requirements) or exploiting existing ethnic and political tensions and widening existing gaps, or through actively fomenting crises that would challenge western organizations and draw upon their resources.

Russia is exploiting democratic deficiency of those states in an effort to gain greater geopolitical influence. The Kremlin seeks to weaken democratic transitions, to erode state institutions and the rule of law concept. To achieve its goals, Moscow looks for shadowy economic deals, encourage corruption and obstruction of justice. It supports political parties and individuals in Europe and the US who challenge the core postulates of liberal democracy and separation of powers.

3. *Need for more intensive cooperation between NATO members and aspiring countries and reliable NATO partners on cyber defense policy*

Increased cooperation between NATO members and aspiring countries on cyber defense policy would be extremely useful. With the adoption of the Talin 2.0 manual by NATO earlier this year, it is imperative that Member States integrate recommendations from the manual in an expedited manner in order to minimize the continued infringement on national sovereignty from online attacks. The United States should be active in partnering with its allies both inside and outside of the alliance. Specifically, by advocating and assisting members to have strong cyber defense policies on a national level, in addition to striving to find stronger paths of communication regarding cyber threats inside of the alliance

Chairman BURR. Thank you, Mr. Ambassador.
Mr. Sarts.

STATEMENT OF JANIS SARTS, DIRECTOR, NATO STRATEGIC COMMUNICATION CENTER OF EXCELLENCE

Mr. SARTS. Thank you, Mr. Chairman, Vice Chairman.

From the time our Center has been established two and a half years ago, we've been closely watching Russian information operations and influence operations across Europe. We've produced 18 different studies on the methodology, ways how Russia tries to affect the outcomes of our democratic processes and our choices.

In the election process typically there are three venues they try to pursue. First, to support the candidate of their choice. To do that, they use the money and they give the support of all the media, traditional media networks that they are controlling, to the candidate, to the proportion as nowhere near of a normal democratic process, with lies, with fakes, etcetera.

Secondly, they try to get the sensitive information on the other candidates to undermine their credibilities. Typically, they try to achieve it through hacking into the systems, but that is not the only way. They use very large segments of disinformation. Fake news is one of the instruments of choice. They're disseminating that through the same information networks they operate within, but they also use fake news site at the networks. They use trolls, both human as well as robotic, to amplify the message. All of that was seen in the recent French election.

Let me just go through quickly what was the French response and what I think we should take note of. First, there was media cooperation. Media were teaming together, and very different sorts of media teaming together to work to verify what is a factual reality. They were supported by the online activist groups like CrossCheck and also big Internet companies like a Facebook and Google joint effort to make sure that the facts also in the digital space take the preeminence over the falsehoods.

Secondly, they were assuming and knowing they were going to be hacked. There were many hack attempts. And of course, all of us who have been in the cyber-security business know you can design only as strong response as possible. There is always a human factor. So what the French idea has been, they trapped the hackers. They fed them the irrelevant information in large amounts, making the dumped information irrelevant as well.

And thirdly, that was how both media, public, and the authorities treated the hack. First, the authorities, based on the French law, said it is illegal to use these hacks for further circulation.

Secondly, most of the media refrained for going for these hacks, understanding the way they are trying to be manipulated into the election process.

Based on that, I'll share some recommendations. First, societal awareness. That is a critical thing to be achieved. The nation that is aware it's under attack is far more resilient than the one that is oblivious of that.

Secondly, as demonstrated by the French case, working with the media is essential, both for their role, but also for their understanding how they might be manipulated in the process.

Thirdly, we still treat it, the information environment, as a game of golf. It is not any more. It's rugby. In rugby, you need to have a very good situational awareness. We have to build tools to know what are the echo chambers, what are the information bubbles, who is trying to penetrate them, what are the robotic networks trying to push, what are the third parties or the outside governments, what kind of data they're looking into your social, societal systems. That is one of the key elements that we have to possess to be able to respond effectively to that game of rugby.

Next, cyber defense. It is a must. Every single element of the election process has to be able to do a good cyber defense, both with two elements, the technical piece and the human piece. These have to be there.

And lastly, we cannot succeed if we don't work together with the technology companies. That's the area where most of the activity takes place and where it is most successful. And I think we can make them one of the good partners in making sure that the facts and truths are much more preeminent in that environment than any falsehood.

Lastly, Mr. Chairman and Mr. Vice Chairman, the reason the Russian activity succeeds is because we have not paid attention. They're using their old tricks and borrowed know-how from our technologies and our marketing know-how. Therefore, I see no reason why they should keep winning. To me, it's about focusing on the problem, bringing different actors across a society together, and then collectively I do believe we have all the potential to win this for us.

Thank you.

[The prepared statement of Mr. Sarts follows:]

**Prepared Statement of Janis Sarts, Director of
NATO Strategic Communications Centre of Excellence**

on

**Russian Interference in European Elections
United States Senate Select Committee on Intelligence**

June 28, 2017

Thank you, Mr. Chairman, Mr. Vice Chairman, for the opportunity to share my views on Kremlin influence operations in Europe, as well as present some ideas on how to counter these risks and develop social resilience to disinformation attacks.

Background

Before exploring this subject, I would like to tell you about the work done at the NATO Strategic Communications Centre of Excellence. The Centre is a NATO accredited international institution created by 11 countries to assist NATO and its allied governments in the development of strategic communications capacities. The Centre is not part of the NATO command structure and is guided by the 11 nations sponsoring the Centre. Thus any views expressed by me as Director are the views of the Centre and do not represent NATO's position as agreed by its 29 member nations.

Our work is centered on researching the phenomenon of information warfare through case studies, lessons learned, and experimentation. Over the past two years we have produced 18 studies that examine different angles of Russian information operations. Based on this research we develop methodologies and techniques that can be employed by NATO and its allies to counter such activities.

The use of influence operations has a long history. During the Cold War the USSR frequently referred to them as "active measures". Thanks to the documents and personal stories that became available during the 1990s, we can now verify that the KGB was primarily responsible for implementing such active measures. It has only been in the last decade that these methodologies have come to be prioritized in Kremlin. After a series of recent failures, including faulty information management during Russia's incursion into Georgia in 2008 and the protests in 2011 that followed V. Putin's bid for a third presidential term, the active measures developed by the KGB have returned to the forefront.

In early 2013 Russian Army General Valeriy Gerasimov described the elements of a new type of conflict where information confrontation is the central element central to all six phases of conflict evolution as defined by the Russian army. In a statement to the Russian State Duma in 2017, Russian Defense Minister Shoigu confirmed that Russia has established information warfare troops within the state security structure.

Tools

The tools Kremlin now uses in its influence operations are a combination of the tools used by the KGB during the Cold War and new elements that exploit our growing technological dependencies. Traditional media outlets are still extensively used to promote Kremlin propaganda within the context of larger influence operations. It is worth noting that the overwhelming majority of Russian news media, reporting within Russia and abroad, are under the direct or indirect control of the Kremlin.

Traditional influence techniques are still in use today. There are many recent examples of news manipulation in the Russian media. During the peak of the European refugee crisis in May 2016, Russia's Channel 24 interviewed locals in France and later reported on these interviews. However, the so-called translations directly contradicted what was actually said in the interviews. In another example, a French school that had been closed for five years was opened to accommodate the refugees; the Russian media reported that the refugees had violently taken over the school. Interviewed French people said they felt safe with the influx of refugees, but the Russian media reported them as saying they felt very frightened.

Today technological developments have vastly increased the reach of information operations. Current online possibilities enable fast, cheap, and geographically unlimited opportunities to spread information. In fact, cyberspace has become a parallel platform for information activities. Actions in virtual space can be used to influence developments in physical space and vice-versa. For example, a well-known information operation, known as the Lisa Case, took place in January of 2016. Many Germans of Russian origin and right-wing extremists went out into streets in Germany to protest the alleged rape of a young Russian girl in response to reports that the alleged perpetrator was a refugee. In fact, there was no rape, but fake information had been convincingly disseminated via social media.

The newest additions to this list include robotic tools such as bots, trolls, and "like-machines". Robotic trolling is coordinated activity by fake accounts in digital media. We can say that at least 8%[1] of Twitter accounts and 5-11%[2] of Facebook accounts are actually bot accounts. The activity of the bots can vary depending on the effect the manager of a bot or troll network wants to achieve with regard to a particular issue. As with any information activity, the goal of robotic trolling is not to persuade but to confuse. Nevertheless, some social media users may perceive emotional and fact-free comments as trustworthy, especially when they are often repeated and appeal to the convictions of those individuals.

Most of these activities seek to exploit preexisting vulnerabilities such as prejudice against minorities, social inequality, migration and corruption. They disrupt normal political processes and to establish an "information fog" that undermines the ability of societies to establish a factual reality.

Cases

Increasingly Kremlin has learned that election periods provide excellent opportunities to use their tools of influence. Properly deployed, these tools have the potential to directly affect the political landscape of the country in question, and, consequently, policies important to Russian interests. Although some cases have been recorded before 2008, Kremlin's meddling in elections intensified after Russia's incursion into Georgia and peaked after anti-Russia sanctions were imposed following annexation of Crimea. It appears that election meddling is

---

[1] Twitter Has Stopped Updating Its Public Tally Of Bots, William Alden, BuzzFeed, 10 November 2015. https://www.buzzfeed.com/williamalden/twitter-has-stopped-updating-its-public-tally-of-bots
[2] Facebook estimates that between 5.5% and 11.2% of accounts are fake, Emil Protalinski, The Next Web, http://thenextweb.com/facebook/2014/02/03/facebook-estimates-5-5-11-2-accounts-fake/

done to either promote candidates friendly to Kremlin or those trying to undermine the EU and NATO and hurt the candidates Kremlin perceives as undesirable.

Election meddling is primarily conducted through:

- Financing pro-Russian candidates and political parties and offering the Kremlin media as platform (Estonian EP elections 2009, French Presidential elections 2017)
- Cyber-attacks against candidates Russia perceives as unfriendly
- Malicious disinformation using social media bots and Kremlin-aligned fringe media outlets

There have been numerous cases in Europe where local authorities have publicly stated that Russia has tried to influence election outcomes.

In 2009 in Estonia: KAPO, the Estonian special service, stated that Russian special services were trying to influence the 2009 European Parliamentary election in Estonia in a way that would lead to the election of a Kremlin-friendly to the European Parliament.

In 2014 in Ukraine: "Fancy Bear Malware" was used to infect the servers at Ukraine's central election commission ahead of the election to declare the Right Sector candidate Dmytro Yarosh as the winner.

In 2015 in Germany: The Russian hacker group APT28 hacked into the German Bundestag, which caused fear that the stolen information could be used to influence the vote in 2017. Hans-Georg Maassen, head of the BfV agency responsible for cyber security said "Our counterpart [in Russia] is trying to generate information that can be used for disinformation or for influence operations".

In 2016 in Montenegro: Montenegro's prosecutors accused Moscow of orchestrating a coup attempt during Montenegro's October 16 election in a bid to stop the country from joining NATO. "So far we have had evidence that Russian nationalist structures were behind [the plot], but now also that Russian state bodies were involved at a certain level," said prosecutor Milivoje Katnic, according to AFP.

In Norway in 2017: Russia-linked hackers attacked government ministries and an anti-Russian political party.

In the Netherlands in 2017: Domestic intelligence officials reported that foreign countries, notably Russia, have tried hundreds of times in recent months to penetrate the computers of government agencies.

The most recent case was during the presidential elections in France: The Kremlin's strategy was to support Marine Le Pen, and do anything to discredit her opponents. This included providing her party, the National Front, with Russian financial backing. In 2014 the National Front received € 9.4 million paid out by the First Czech-Russian Bank and signed an additional loan application with the Russian NKB bank on 15 June 2016. The last loan of 3 million euros was "intended to finance the French election campaign". In the run up to the elections in March 2017 there was a surprise meeting between Marine Le Pen and Vladimir Putin that received broad coverage by Russian media, including the French outlets of RT and Sputnik.

Sputnik and RT published rumors of the "double life" of Emmanuel Macron, saying that he is supported by a "very rich gay lobby". Since its launch, Macron's party *En marche!* has undergone more than 2500 intrusion attempts, including 907 from the Ukraine. These cyber-attacks "suddenly increased" in January, when the election polls showed increasing popular support of Macron.

The Atlantic Council's Digital Forensic Research Lab has tracked down networks of bots involved in promoting the candidates favored by Russia in various elections including Geert Wilders in the Dutch general election campaign and Marine Le Pen in the French Presidential election campaign. Although their connection to the Kremlin cannot be confirmed, the narrative spread by the bots was identical to that of the Kremlin-funded media, and synergies between two were frequent and consistent.

Response

First turning point for NATO and European NATO allies was the annexation of Crimea by Russia and the start of the conflict in Eastern Ukraine. NATO developed strategy for countering hybrid warfare, NATO nations established Strategic Communications Centre of Excellence in 2014.

In order to confront Russian information confrontation NATO is applying 2 different approaches. First of all NATO invests extra time and effort to inform and to explain its home audience as well as outside audiences about NATO goals and actions. NATO narrative of collective defense and security should be circulated and showed by NATO's deeds first of all by NATO itself. And that is what NATO does. Subsequent monitoring and assessment of how your narrative resonates with expectations and perceptions of your target audiences are important for further strategic communication of NATO.

Other track which NATO undertakes is an assessment of hostile information activities against NATO. Current NATO operations have additional focus on information environment assessment of the operation theater. That includes identification, tracking, monitoring and analyzing of hostile information activities. It is a new capability which is being developed via several tracks simultaneously and includes current operations, concept development of information environment assessment tools and processes and development of the new NATO capability. Also the newest NATO mission –"Enhanced Forward Presence" of allied troops in Estonia, Latvia, Lithuania and Poland is faced with the increased amounts of false information, starting with allegedly raped teenage girl by German soldiers' case in Lithuania, to Canada sending "gay" battalion to Latvia. NATO has put in place mechanisms to address and counter these information attacks effectively.

European governments have also started to increasingly address the problem of Russian disinformation and influence operations. I see three generic tracks that are being pursued: organizational, capability development and work with the society.

Typically foreign influence operations are handled by the special services within the countries, but increased public nature of these activities have limited the effectiveness of the tools that can be deployed by these institutions to counter the challenge. More and more the response has also to be public and immediate. Increasingly governments choose to give the principal coordination responsibility to the central element of executive power – prime minister. In countries such as Finland, Estonia, Latvia and Poland central government body has people tasked with coordination and implementing the response to these threats. In other countries Sweden, Czech Republic, Lithuania agencies are given new responsibilities and resources in this area.

Secondly, more resources are being devoted to develop capabilities in two essential response areas- cyber defence and strategic communications. In large majority of European nations there is a growing trend to invest more in one or both of these elements. Germany recently created a new Cyber Command as part of their military system, countries are also increasingly investing in their military and nonmilitary strategic communications capabilities including new information flow monitoring systems.

Thirdly, as most of the influence attacks aim at changing society's perceptions and thus behavior models, governments increasingly work with civic society, to build necessary resilience. Increased funding for investigative journalism, and objective journalism, increased media literacy, work with fact checking groups are just some of the lines of effort taken by European nations. As the result, in some countries there is increased activity by citizens to engage and counter disinformation, the most prominent being so called " Elves" in Lithuania and Latvia- groups of civic activists that fight ' Trolls " and their messages in online environment.

Recommendations

Raising society's awareness. As has been described before, society and its perceptions are the main targets of the contemporary influence operations. Accordingly, one of the key resilience mechanisms, our research shows, is awareness of the society of being targeted by third party malicious actors to affect their election behavior. We have seen resilience levels raise instantly as society recognizes being targeted by outside actor.

To accomplish it working with the media is one of the key parameters. Not only it is the key tool to uncover the potential fakes and strategies to undermine cohesion of social processes, media are usually manipulated by Kremlin, by understanding their instinctive reactions to "sensational" material , as tools in the given influence operation. I believe, France presidential election second round and the reaction of the main French media in the run-up to the electoral vote is one of the good examples of media response through understanding how they are used in the attempts to impact last minute election choices.

Situational awareness. In the modern information environment the old monitoring techniques are far from sufficient. If society is under outside influence attack, it has to use the tools that enable the situational awareness of the information space that correspond to that what we require of more traditional battle space. What kind of information bubbles (eco cambers) society consists of? Do we see foreign influence in these bubbles? What kind of narratives, hashtags, in support of which foreign actors are the robotic networks pushing? To what end? Is our citizens' data being sucked out by outside actors? These are just some questions that in the new information environment we have to be able to answer to keep our enemies at bay.

Cyber defence. In the western methodology we tend to see and approach cyber world as that of algorithms, networks, data clouds and machines. We forget that increasing number of the cyber-attacks through the technical world attack human consciousness either through typical phishing attack or more complex influence operation. Still it is and will increasingly be important to build cyber resilience both within technical contexts, but increasingly within human context.

Working with the technology companies. As I have argued before, most of the Kremlin influence techniques are comparatively old, what has enabled their new efficiency is the different information environment where the confrontation takes place. The new technology platforms are the place where most of these methods are most efficient. I would argue, that it is not the technologies fault, but mostly how they interact with human mind. We should increasingly work with the tech companies to counter the disinformation trend. We have to see the ways we can use the new technologies to help and educate our societies to distinguish fact from fiction, normal social debate from foreign influence, a real human from a robotic program used to push the subject.

Finally Mr Chairman, Mr Vice Chairman. The influence operations Kremlin is pursuing are based on old soviet techniques combined with clever use of our technologies and increasingly of our marketing knowhow. I see no reason why we should be losing. It is about acknowledging the problem, resourcing solutions and using that is best in our societies (free speech, civic engagement, innovation) to win it for our future.

Chairman BURR. Thank you, Mr. Sarts.
Dr. Stelzenmueller.

STATEMENT OF DR. CONSTANZE STELZENMUELLER, BOSCH SENIOR FELLOW, BROOKINGS INSTITUTION

Dr. STELZENMUELLER. Thank you and good morning. Chairman Burr, Vice Chairman Warner, distinguished members of this Committee: It's an honor for me to be invited here today to testify before you on the critical issue before this panel, Russian interference on the European elections and specifically on the federal election on September 24 in my country, Germany.

Russian interference in the European political space is strategic and is aimed at destabilizing the European project. Germany is the fulcrum with which to achieve this goal. Weaken Germany and you diminish the E.U. and the European project. And conversely, because Germany has orchestrated the European consensus on sanctions against Russia, it has become the main obstacle for Russia in pursuing its interest in Europe and Ukraine.

Russian interference in Germany, as we know, has occurred for a long time. It is not limited to these elections, nor will it stop thereafter. As for the election itself, there is a general consensus in my country that there will be meddling; the only question is when and in what form that will take.

Technical manipulation of the elections, however, is unlikely. We use paper ballots and we have hardened the computer infrastructure that we use to aggregate the data. The real target of Russian interference in Germany is voters' heads. They're trying to hack our political consciousness. For this, they use a broad spectrum of tools, from propaganda, to disinformation, to hacking and denial-of-service attacks to, of course, more classical means, such as individual or institutional agents of influence.

Attribution and intent, of course, remain elusive. This is one of the most difficult problems, not least because not even the Russian authorities ordering interference are monolithic or cohesive. And execution is often outsourced or delegated, including to what President Putin has called "patriotic hackers."

The impact of Kremlin interference, if we're honest here, is also hit and miss, often miss. In many ways, its meddling in European elections over the past year has produced the exact opposite of what was intended. It has produced stable, democratic, and non-populist governments that are pro-European Union and indeed pro-NATO and pro-American. The populists have lost out almost everywhere and NATO and the E.U., I'm happy to say, are experiencing a renaissance of purpose. And in the German race, what looked a neck-to-neck race for a while at the beginning of the year is now looking quite different. Chancellor Merkel is holding a steady 14-point lead.

But that does not mean—and I urge you to consider this—that Russia cannot still do significant damage.

As for countermeasures, Germany has certainly taken a while to take note of the threat, but it has been making up, racing to make up for lost time over the past two years by hardening its defenses and creating more resilience. That's not to say there's still not much more to be done, particularly on the civil society front. And

German politicians certainly need to do better at articulating their narrative against Kremlin disinformation.

And, of course, it helps that Germany is not the first country to face this threat. In fact, we come at the end of a long string of elections, and we can learn from our friends and allies, particularly from the French case just explained by Janis Sarts.

That said, we have no reason whatsoever as Germans or as Europeans to be complacent. In fact, the successes of Russian interference, such as they are, are a measure of our failures and we need to examine those.

Now, what form could Russian interference in the September 24 elections take? Obviously, if there were a major terrorist attack, if there were a return of the refugee crisis, that could be exploited by propaganda. It's conceivable that there would be further severe DDoS attacks, or further hacks or, in fact, a leak of the 2015 hack substance. Sixteen gigabytes were taken away; we haven't seen them yet.

But it is just as likely that a visible Russian attempt to use such events would backfire, as it has before. So they need to tread carefully there. And interference could just as well take the form of ongoing careful probing and testing of our vulnerabilities, combined with a continuous slow drip of toxic disinformation, as is happening now, all the time.

So Germany will have to remain vigilant, but also flexible and relaxed. We mustn't overdramatize the scope, intent, or coherence of the threat. That would be to walk in to the main psychological threat of this propaganda, which is to think the threat is bigger than it actually is. We are a strong and vibrant democracy and we can fight this in the marketplace, too. However, it is beyond any doubt that Germany and all of Europe are experiencing a phase of historical volatility and drift. And in such a time, friends and allies matter more than ever. And here, our relationship with America, is key.

We understand that Europe needs to do more for its own defense and take on more of the burden of transatlantic security relationship off the United States. And we have, as many here know, and as Nick knows, we have already taken many steps towards this goal. But the alliance as such, our political, economic, military, and intelligence partnership, is crucial for the preservation of the European project. And an America that feels ambiguous about the value of this alliance could be perceived by the Kremlin as the ultimate encouragement.

I therefore respectfully have only one recommendation for you, or rather it is a request: Stand by us.

Thank you very much and I look forward to your questions.

[The prepared statement of Dr. Stelzenmueller follows:]

BROOKINGS

The Impact of Russian Interference on Germany's 2017 Elections

Dr. Constanze Stelzenmüller

Robert Bosch Senior Fellow, Center on the United States and Europe

Brookings Institution

Testimony before the U.S. Senate Select Committee on Intelligence

Wednesday, June 28, 2017

Chairman Burr, Vice Chairman Warner, distinguished members of the Senate Select Committee on Intelligence,

It is an honor for me to be invited to testify before you here today on the critical issue before this panel: the impact of Russian interference on European elections, and more particularly in my case, on the German federal elections on September 24.

The question of how to deal with Russian attempts to influence our polities has become one of the most salient policy questions of our time. But Europeans have been working to detect, evaluate, and counter this kind of meddling for many years now.[1]

1. It's about the West: Russian active measures are strategic

Three things are new about Russian interference today. *Firstly*, it appears to be directed not just at Europe's periphery, or at specific European nations like Germany, but at destabilizing the European project from the inside out: dismantling decades of progress toward building a democratic Europe that is whole, free, and at peace. *Secondly*, its covert and overt "active measures" are much more diverse, larger-scale, and more technologically sophisticated; they continually adapt and morph in accordance with changing technology and circumstances. *Thirdly*, by striking at Europe and the United States at the same time, the interference appears to be geared towards undermining the effectiveness and cohesion of the Western alliance as such—and at the legitimacy of the West as a normative force upholding a global order based on universal rules rather than might alone.

That said, Russia's active measures are presumably directed at a domestic audience as much as towards the West: They are designed to show that Europe and the U.S. are no alternative to Putin's Russia. Life under Putin, the message runs, may be less than perfect; but at least it is stable.

2. Germany is the prize: Berlin currently leads Europe, including on relations with Russia

The past year has seen a string of key European elections: the Italian constitutional referendum on December 4, 2016, the election in the Netherlands on March 15 of this year, the French presidential (April 23 and May 7) and legislative (June 11 and 18) votes, and the British polls on June 8. But arguably none is quite as consequential for the future of Europe as the September 24 federal elections in Germany, in which Chancellor Angela Merkel is running for a fourth term.

Notwithstanding the recent French presidential election victory of Emmanuel Macron, a passionate European who appears determined to be a strong leader as well as an ally to chancellor Angela Merkel, Germany remains a major power, and in some ways *the* fulcrum of power on the continent. For a Russia that is clearly bent on destabilizing Europe and the transatlantic alliance, Germany is the prize: Weaken Germany, and you diminish the EU and the European project.

Russia's antagonism towards Germany is a relatively recent development. The two countries share an age-old, deep, and strong relationship, a tangle of reciprocal interests and exchanges, but also a legacy of victimization and complicity; never more than in the 20th century. The memory of that guilt will forever be part of Germany's cultural DNA. Yet in the fateful years of 1989-90, Germany and its then-chancellor Helmut Kohl had cause to be grateful to Soviet President Mikhail Gorbachev's enlightened decision to drop support for the East German regime, and to agree to the reunification of a divided Germany as well as to the peaceful withdrawal of Soviet troops from East German territory.

A year later, the dissolution of the USSR and the Warsaw Pact set in motion a chain of events that led to the enlargement of NATO and the EU: "Europe whole and free" meant an immense increase of prosperity and security for all of Europe, but for none more than Germany. For two decades thereafter, Germany was seen in the Kremlin as a friend and ally, as a partner in modernizing the Russian economy, especially through German manufacturing exports and investment, and as a strategic bridgehead into Europe—not least because Germany was importing roughly a third of its oil and gas from Russia.

German attitudes were somewhat more ambiguous. Germany wanted Russia as a partner, and hoped that it might guide it towards a transformation similar to the one undergone by Eastern Europe. Its "modernization partnership" with Russia had been based on two implicit assumptions: firstly, that economic integration would be reciprocal and, secondly, that it would lead to gradual political transformation in Russia, which would bring it closer to Europe. But economic integration turned out to be strictly downstream; and political reform remained elusive. When then-President Dmitry Medvedev called for a "new European security architecture" in a June 5, 2008 speech in the German capital, it became clear to senior German policymakers that Moscow was still hoping to put NATO out of business and push the U.S. out of Europe. Many in Berlin placed the blame for the Russo-Georgian war in August of the same year on Georgian President Mikheil Saakashvili rather than the Kremlin; nonetheless, Germans were deeply alarmed by Russia's actions and its increasing antagonism toward NATO, as well as the EU. The relationship with Moscow soured from then on.

Between 2008 and 2014, a string of events pushed Germany into the role of a "reluctant hegemon" (*The Economist*) in Europe. The global financial crisis, which swiftly became a Eurozone crisis, exacerbated an already existing economic north-south divide in Europe, and led to the rise of populist parties and movements across the continent. Systemic competition between the EU and Russia in Europe's eastern neighborhood became increasingly apparent. And there was growing turmoil in Northern Africa and the Middle East in the wake of the Libya intervention and the short-lived "Arab spring." A U.S. administration announcing retrenchment in Europe and a "pivot to Asia," French introspection, and the looming specter of a Brexit: all contributed to a recognition in Berlin that the European project was in peril, and that Germany, now Europe's leader by default, would have to step up to the challenge of preserving it. At the Munich Security Conference in January 2014, Germany's president as well as its foreign and defense ministers called for a more responsible and forward-leaning

German foreign policy. Subsequent institutional reforms, key policy documents, and responses to events like the refugee crisis have demonstrated the seriousness of their resolve.

This backdrop of growing regional volatility and risk, and Germany's decision to rise to the challenge of leadership, is essential for understanding Germany's role in the ensuing Ukraine crisis, which redefined Berlin's relationship with Moscow. Russia's illegal annexation of Crimea following the Euromaidan uprising, the downing of Malaysian Airlines flight MH-17, and Russia's continuing support of conflict in eastern Ukraine, as well as Moscow's campaign of lies, bullying, and propaganda, made German policymakers realize that their offers of de-escalation and "off-ramps" were not being reciprocated. They concluded that they were facing a Russian policy based on confrontation rather than cooperation.

The chancellor, as well as her former and current foreign ministers Frank Walter Steinmeier and Sigmar Gabriel, reacted by announcing that the "strategic relationship" with Russia is over for the foreseeable future. Germany has been leading negotiations with Russia and Ukraine in the "Minsk Process," and it has orchestrated and held together the European consensus on sanctions against Russia. These actions make Berlin the main obstacle for Russia in pursuing its interests in Europe and Ukraine.[2]

Finally, Chancellor Merkel is one of the few Western leaders who can understand, and speak to, Vladimir Putin in his own language; by all accounts, she does so calmly and fearlessly. Merkel has been at pains to deprecate attempts to depict her as the "beacon of the free world"; but they are unlikely to have endeared her to Russia's prickly president. For Putin, humbling Merkel would be a victory for him across Europe, and the West. Small wonder that she, and Germany, are the object of the Kremlin's particular hostility today.

3. It's not just about elections: Russian interference will continue

A divided Germany was Ground Zero for espionage, propaganda, and other kinds of influence operations throughout the Cold War; this did not end with the fall of the Berlin Wall. Experts identify Vladimir Putin's return to the Russian presidency in 2000 as the beginning of a much more systematic gearing up of influence operations directed at Europe and Germany—with a noticeable increase following Germany's decision to support Ukraine's efforts to attach itself to Europe. In the words of the most recent annual domestic intelligence report published by the German Interior Ministry (it oversees the domestic intelligence agency *Bundesamt für Verfassungsschutz,* or Office for the Protection of the Constitution) of 2015: "With their broad-based efforts to acquire information and exercise influence, the Russian intelligence services have been active for many years with high intensity against German interests in Germany and in the Russian Federation ... there is no reason to assume that their espionage activities will abate in the foreseeable future."[3]

4. We get it: Germans are concerned about Russian interference

Senior German officials have been notably more explicit than many of their European peers in attributing cyber hacks and other forms of interference to Russia. Chancellor Angela Merkel has publicly acknowledged that the German government is concerned about Russian active measures, and raised the issue in person with Russian President Vladimir Putin at a recent meeting in Sochi.[4] The head of the (external) Federal Intelligence Service (*Bundesnachrichtendienst/BND*), Bruno Kahl,[5] and the head of the domestic intelligence service Office for the Protection of the Constitution (*Bundesamt für Verfassungsschutz/BfV*), Hans-Georg Maaßen, have repeatedly confirmed that their agencies are on the lookout for Russian meddling.[6] The aforementioned annual report on domestic intelligence notes in its chapter on Russian measures that besides espionage at a "high organizational and financial volume," Russian intelligence services are also "attempting to influence Germany's decisionmakers and public opinion."[7]

The topic has been prominent on the radar of German think tanks and media for the past three years—roughly coinciding with the annexation of Crimea and the beginning of large-scale Russian trolling in German social media.[8]

Heightened awareness in Germany is due to several high-profile cases of active measures in Germany, but also to the salience of the issue in the United States, in France, and elsewhere in Europe. (Trust in Russia has plummeted in German public opinion surveys; German-Russian relations are perceived overwhelmingly as bad; and there has been consistently high support for sanctions based on Russia's role in Ukraine.)

As for the September 24 elections, there seems to be a broad consensus in Berlin that Russia will attempt to meddle with the decision of the voters. The only open questions are when, and what form that interference will take. Less than two weeks ago, Germany's President (and former foreign minister) Frank Walter Steinmeier weighed in. Remarking on "a decade and a half of growing alienation between Europe and Russia," he warned: "If Moscow interferes with the Bundestag elections, (...) that would be damaging for both sides."[9]

5. It's not a hardware threat: Technical manipulation of Germany's elections is unlikely

Germany does not use voting machines; citizens vote on paper ballots. The Federal Statistical Office (*Statistisches Bundesamt),* which oversees elections, employs computers to process and aggregate the data. But it uses an encrypted network that is not connected to the internet. Its president Dieter Sarreither has told the media that the entire network infrastructure has been overhauled and modernized since the last election in 2013. Together with the Federal Office for Security in Information Technology (*Bundesamt für Sicherheit in der Informationstechnik/BSI*), his agency has been conducting regular simulations, such as "attempts to invade our system and discover potential weak spots."[10]

A hacking of voting technology in the German elections probably can't be excluded completely; but experts concur it is highly unlikely to succeed. Voters' heads are by far the more vulnerable target.

6. The toolbox of head-hacking: Russian interference occurs on a broad spectrum

Propaganda: The three key German-language propaganda outlets linked to the Kremlin are RT Deutsch, Sputnik Deutsch, and NewsFront Deutsch, which appeared on the German market in 2013. The two former are funded and managed by the Kremlin; the latter claims to be independent, but as the analyst Ben Nimmo has pointed out,[11] its editorial stance matches that of the Kremlin, and it is reported to be funded by the Russian secret services.[12] None of the three are major players in the German media market, whether in terms of output or of followers.[13] Their disproportionate impact derives from highly active pushers or amplifiers. Some of these are automated (bots) or semi-automated (cyborgs). Others are human networks, often connected to either pro-Russian or far-right and anti-migrant groups, particularly the Alternative for Germany (*Alternative für Deutschland/AfD*) party. Extreme left- and right-wing conspiracy media outlets (Jürgen Elsässer's magazine *Compact*, the Kopp publishing house) help in adopting and amplifying Russian narratives.

For Germany's Russian-German community,[14] estimated at around 2.5 million people,[15] the original Russian-language state media—which for years have been waging a relentless campaign against a "Gayropa" of extreme liberal values and overrun by swarthy Muslim migrants, and other tropes of a decadent West—also remain an important source of information. That said, this community is often caricatured as monolithically conservative, which risks scapegoating it unfairly as a passive or even willing victim of manipulation.

Disinformation: The most famous case of disinformation pushed by Russian outlets is that of "Our Lisa," the supposed abduction and rape of an underage Russian-German girl in January 2016 by three men variously identified as "Muslim" or "Arab." The groundless reports caused hundreds of Russian-Germans to demonstrate in cities across Germany, including in front of the Chancellery in Berlin. In many ways, this was Germany's wake-up call, coming as it did at a time when German public opinion was on edge from the impact of nearly a million refugees, and during three regional election campaigns.

In 2014, Russian media blamed the crash of Malaysian Airlines flight MH-17—which Western officials said was shot down by Russian-supported separatists with a Russian-supplied missile—on Ukrainian fighters; in general, they have depicted Ukraine's politicians as corrupt, fascist, or both. Another false story in January 2017 alleged that German Bundeswehr soldiers had raped a young girl while stationed in Lithuania as part of a NATO reassurance mission. Other reports said that 700,000 Germans had left the country because of Merkel's refugee policy, or that refugees had destroyed the oldest church in Germany. A video portraying the German chancellor as mentally ill received more than a million views.[16] Other narratives of Russian disinformation focus on alleged U.S. and NATO aggression, migrants and refugees, and radical Islam.

Hacking and denial-of-service attacks: In January 2015, the pro-Russian hacker group CyberBerkut undertook a two-day DDOS (distributed denial of service) attack on German government computers—timed precisely to coincide with a visit of Ukrainian Prime Minister Arseniy Yatsenyuk; the hackers called "all Germans and the German government to end financial aid for the criminal government in Kiev." In April and May 2015, the German federal legislature (*Bundestag*) came under sustained attack by hackers over several weeks. They infected a network that includes more than 5,600 computers and 12,000 registered users (including those of at least 16 members of the Bundestag and chancellor Merkel's office) with malware, and stole 16 gigabytes of data in what has been the most extensive and damaging cyberattack on German government institutions so far. The attack was so severe that the entire Bundestag network had to be taken offline for four days. In response, Merkel spoke of "hybrid warfare." German domestic intelligence blamed the attack on the group known as APT28 (also known as Fancy Bear or Pawn Storm), which is thought to be linked to the Russian GRU, or military intelligence; it is also believed to have executed the hack on the Democratic National Convention's servers in July 2016 with the purpose of discrediting the Clinton campaign. According to news reports, in a 2016 unpublished analysis commissioned by the Chancellery, the German intelligence agencies concluded that it should be assumed that cyber hacks such as these are directly authorized by the President's Office in the Kremlin.[17]

Other potential channels of Russian influence operations: these include "agents of influence" who promote Russian interests and narratives willingly or unwittingly ("useful idiots"), be they politicians, academics, businessmen, or journalists. Russia has recruited senior German politicians like former chancellor Gerhard Schröder, who took a position as the board chairman of the Nord Stream pipeline project, or Matthias Warnig, a former Stasi (East German domestic intelligence) officer who is now the CEO of the pipeline consortium. The "Ostausschuss" (Eastern Committee) of the German Federation of Industry, is the main lobbying organization for German companies operating in Russia and a traditional voice for pro-Russian business interests. Then there are convening fora such as the "Petersburger Dialog" (funded mostly by the German foreign ministry), and the "Deutsch-Russisches Forum" (funded mainly by the business community). These were once set up to transfer Western values eastwards to post-Soviet Russia; today, critics say, they work the other way around. In June 2016, they were supplemented with a high-profile Russian export, the first of its kind in Berlin: the "Dialogue of Civilizations" research institute set up by the Yakunin Foundation.

The Left (*Die Linke*) party on the extreme left and the AfD on the extreme right regularly voice overt, sometimes even enthusiastic, support for Kremlin positions. The extremist anti-migrant and anti-Islam movement Pegida also trumpets its allegiance to Moscow; Russian flags have been seen at its rallies.

The center-left Social Democratic party (SPD) is often accused outside Germany of being a homogeneous bloc of *Putinversteher*, or Putin-sympathizers. The main reason for this is its long-standing support of *Ostpolitik*, a policy of rapprochement with the soviet Union and then Russia that—despite its undoubted historic merit as a framework for balancing détente with deterrence during the Cold War—today more often than not is invoked to condone accommodation and equidistancing.

Yet this charge is doubly simplistic. For one, the SPD is increasingly torn on Russia, and numerous Social Democrats are highly critical of the Kremlin's policies. And *Putinversteher* can be found across the established party spectrum—including in Angela Merkel's own center-right Christian Democrats or (even more noticeably) in its Bavarian sister party, the Christian Social Union (CSU). In Germany, sympathy for the Kremlin's authoritarian rule is more often a function of cultural conservatism, anti-Americanism, or negative attitudes to globalization and European integration, than of party political preference. More simply put: These cleavages run though all the parties and their voter bases, except those on the extreme left and right fringes.

7. Attribution is elusive: No "smoking gun," but plenty of firearms out there

The 2015 domestic intelligence report notes drily that "in most cases" it is difficult to establish direct attribution of interference by Russian intelligence agencies; yet it bluntly states that such attempts take place all the time.[18] The heads of the German intelligence services have confirmed this repeatedly in recent months—while at the same time being careful to say that there is no "smoking gun."

Also, while German experts see Russian state authorities giving quite specific and detailed orders and instructions regarding interference, they note that there appears to be rivalry and competition within the system—including in the intelligence services. Moreover, execution is more often than not loosely organized, and delegated to a broad variety of actors. Some are tied closely into a chain of command, others are linked much more tenuously to government authorities—e.g. subcontractors, businessmen, hacking organizations (Vladimir Putin's "patriotic hackers"), freelancers, and even organized cybercrime networks. Russia expert Mark Galeotti calls this a "multidirectional brush-fire-information-warfare campaign"—as opposed to the single overarching conspiracy many observers seem to fear, and also quite unlike the "ruthless centralized command and control of the Soviet model."[19]

This method allows for maximum agility, speed, adaptability, and creativity. It permits proceeding by trial and error. And it allows state actors to evade attribution, and retaliation. That said, it can also mean a sacrifice of control and effectiveness, increasing the likelihood of mistakes, and leading to different actors operating at cross-purposes, perhaps even canceling each other out—as when Kremlin-directed propaganda portrays Ukrainians as nationalists without a nation, or simultaneously controlled by Jews and Nazis.

8. Sowing the fields with salt: Russian interference is destructive, not constructive

There is wide agreement among German experts that the Kremlin's goal is not to help a particular candidate or party to victory. According to Bruno Kahl, the head of the external intelligence agency, the aim is "delegitimizing the democratic process as such. No matter whom they help get ahead."[20]

No doubt the intent to damage includes Chancellor Merkel and other political leaders of political parties. But more generally, the purpose of Russian interference in the arena of German public opinion appears to be to shatter Germans' confidence in the stability and integrity of their country and its institutions, as well as to sow confusion, doubt, and distrust. Or, as Mark Galeotti writes about the Kremlin's meddling in the 2016 U.S. elections: it "was not to elect the supposedly unelectable Trump, but to sow the fields with salt for Hillary Clinton."[21]

9. Russian interference is hit-and-miss: the question (and questionableness) of impact

Because of the attribution problem, assessing the precise impact of Russian interference is a difficult enterprise. But so far, the impact of Russian active measures in Europe appears to have been somewhat hit-and-miss—with an emphasis on "miss." Certainly none of the past year's elections has yielded outcomes favorable to the Kremlin; in fact, European voters— possibly spooked by the combination of Brexit, the U.S. election, and France's brush with the *Front National* and Marine le Pen—have been mostly hewing to the mean.

NATO and the EU, far from crumpling into irrelevance, are experiencing a renaissance of purpose. Most member states have been increasing their defense budgets at rates not seen since the Cold War, and EU security and defense policy has just been given a considerable boost; Montenegro joined the transatlantic military alliance as its 29th member on June 5th. Russian military intervention also ended up tipping the balance in favor of a deeper European engagement with the two countries that were the object of Russia's aggression: Georgia (2008), and Ukraine (2014-present). Ukraine, despite the continuing conflict in Donetsk and Luhansk provinces, and the manifest imperfections of the Minsk process, has become the recipient of significant Western development support and investment, not least from Germany. And both Ukraine and Georgia have just been granted visa-free travel to Europe.

German voters did vote for the AfD in double-digit numbers in several state elections at the height of concerns about refugees last year. But in the three latest state elections (all in 2017), the AfD was back to single-digit numbers.

The national race briefly looked like the kind of neck-to-neck contest where a small amount of interference might actually provide results, when the SPD challenger Martin Schulz pulled ahead of the chancellor in polls at the beginning of the year. However, Merkel has been enjoying a solid 14-point lead for weeks now. The latest national poll has her CDU at 39 percent, the SPD at 24 percent, and the Greens and the Liberals at 8 and 7 percent, respectively. The extreme left *Die Linke* and the rightwing AfD score 9 and 8 percent.[22]

Nor are there currently any leaders on offer who fit the Kremlin mold *and* show a remote chance of winning elections. Martin Schulz, a long-time president of the European Parliament, is deeply committed to the idea of a European destiny for Germany. And unlike France's Marine le Pen, the leaders of *Die Linke* and the AfD—Sahra Wagenknecht on the left, and Alexander Gauland and Frauke Petry (recently ousted by Alice Weidel) on the right—have never managed to develop a broad-based popular appeal. Wagenknecht has flip-flopped repeatedly on the question of whether her party might enter into a coalition with the Social Democrats. The AfD's governance record in the 13 (of 16) state legislatures in which it holds seats has been abysmal. Its leadership has spent most of its energy in ugly public squabbles.

Elsewhere, Kremlin meddling has visibly backfired, producing results that are the opposite of what appears to have been intended. In the "Our Lisa" case, Russian state television had for days whipped itself into a frenzy of indignation about the supposed failure of German authorities to pursue the alleged perpetrators, when foreign minister Sergei Lavrov waded in and accused Germany of obstruction of justice—causing a rare public outburst of anger in his normally unflappable counterpart Frank Walter Steinmeier. Ordinary Germans had already been inundated for many months with a seemingly endless toxic sludge of internet trolling (often with a recognizable Russian syntax) on their social media in response to the Ukraine crisis. To many, the Lisa story merely confirmed the malice and brazenness of Russia's efforts at manipulating public opinion.

The Russia lobby is no longer as powerful in Germany as it used to be—not least because so many German companies have been burned doing business in Russia. German exports to Russia in 2016 account for only 2 percent (down from 4 percent in 2015) of total German exports, and Russia is currently 13th (down from 11th) on the list of Germany's bilateral trade partners.[23]

Germany's media—subject to an even more determined onslaught of abuse—have not been cowed into submission either. Rather, they have responded in much the same way as their French, American, and other counterparts: by adding fact-checking and investigative capabilities, and by taking on the fight. Russian outlets like RT and Sputnik, meanwhile, have had difficulty hiring German-language staff, and their output has consequently been noticeably low-grade. The Yakunin Foundation has also reportedly had difficulty hiring staff for its Berlin operations, despite the promise of substantial paychecks.

For the Merkel government, the Kremlin's interference has validated a tough stance towards Russia, and substantiated the need for improving defenses abroad and resilience at home. This year, Germany's defense budget is set to increase by 8 percent; the chancellor has publicly confirmed several times that Germany intends to meet its NATO commitment to spend two percent of its GDP on defense by the target date of 2024. And it is surely not unkind to speculate that the intelligence services, never particularly popular in Germany, might also derive some welcome (and arguably appropriate) vindication from this situation—not just for their standing, but also for their budgets.

Yet it should be remembered that the confusion and doubt sowed by Russian meddling continue to offer potential opportunities for exploitation, even when the Kremlin loses on a larger goal.[24] In Germany, like elsewhere in the West, there are many people whose preconceptions, attitudes, and fears make them susceptible to such messages.

10. We're on it: Countermeasures

Germany took a long time to wake up to the threat posed by interference and information warfare. In the last three years, however, it has undertaken a lot to harden its defenses and create more resilience:

- Publication of a government cybersecurity strategy (2016);
- Creation of a Cyber Defense Center and a secure government network;
- Creation of a mobile quick reaction force within the Federal Office for Information Security (*Bundesamt für Sicherheit in der Informationstechnik/BSI*);
- Identification of hybrid threats and cyberwarfare as a key security concern in the 2016 German Defense Whitebook;
- Creation of a 13,500 strong Cyber and Information Space Command as the sixth branch of the German armed forces;

- Government institutions and parties have improved their defenses and created rapid response teams;
- Germany's parties have pledged not to employ bots in the election campaign; they are discussing a promise not to exploit any potential last-minute dumps from the parliament hack;
- Think tanks like Stiftung Neue Verantwortung, the Global Public Policy Institute, the German Council on Foreign Relations and the Stiftung Wissenschaft und Politik have been working on analyzing the threat of Russian disinformation and articulating cyberdefense policy;
- New independent media monitoring organizations like Correctiv pursue and call out disinformation;

Public acknowledgement of Russian interference by senior officials is deliberate and aims to both raise the bar for the Kremlin and sensitize the German public; the message has been repeated on visits to Moscow. Immediate evaluation and a calm, measured response—as when the Berlin police immediately stated the "Our Lisa" accusations to be entirely unfounded—is also intended to deter future disinformation attempts.

However, German responses on the whole are very state-centric, and a number of key issues remain unresolved and/or highly controversial:

- The Bundestag (federal legislature) is not connected to the government network, and insists on running its own network(s);
- Institutions seeking to boost their cyberdefense capabilities face a shortage of qualified personnel;
- Public attribution strategy needs to be refined in a way that earns public confidence and delivers on deterrence;
- A draft German law (the *Netzwerkdurchsetzungsgesetz*) seeks to force social media platforms like Facebook, Twitter, and Google to enforce existing hate speech laws and prevent the spread of fake news, threatening them with fines if they do not remove malicious content;[25]
- Several German agencies are thinking about developing offensive countermeasures ("hackback" or "deterrence by retaliation") capabilities—but this raises complex issues of attribution, normative framing, and escalation control;
- Media and cyber literacy as well as safety consciousness in the German public needs to be improved;
- German politicians and policymakers need to do far better at articulating their own narratives clearly and convincingly.

Some of these questions raise larger and very complex constitutional and political issues: the separation of powers, the relationship between state, business and citizens, as well as the proper allocation of responsibility and regulatory authority for securing public institutions and civil society against threats and risks. They also beg the thorny question of how to draw the line between free speech and a threat to/violation of public goods. Where does free speech end, and censorship begin? When, indeed, is "meddling" merely ineffective persuasion or soft power, and when is it a malicious influence operation? How can executive agencies respond adequately to such inchoate threats without overreach? And what is the proper role of the legislative and the judiciary in balancing and reviewing the executive—not least the secret executive? In defining interference as a threat to public safety, how do we as a polity preserve the agency of individual citizens? Finally, engaging the German public on all this in a way that empowers citizens to make the right decisions for their own security will require enormous energy and trust.

11. Germany's strengths and vulnerabilities

In countering Russian meddling, Germany has a number of inherent strengths—strengths that some other countries lack. Its politics are far less polarized than, say those of the United States, or the United Kingdom; income and education inequality is far less drastic than in the Anglo-Saxon world. It has healthy institutions, a functioning representative democracy, and genuine political pluralism. Its economy is strong, its public education good. It possesses a large number of independent, quality media organizations which are still trusted by consumers, and social media are less relevant for public debate than elsewhere.[26] Unemployment is minimal, and crime is low. Germans are generally aware that European integration and globalization have brought them enormous prosperity and security.

It also helps that Germany is not the first country to face this issue in an election. We can learn from the experience of others—not least from France, where policymakers used existing election rules (a pre-vote campaign blackout period) and creative countermeasures (deliberately planted fake news to confuse hackers) to thwart interference. In gauging our overall response to external influencing attempts, we can study a variety of models, from the highly alert posture of the Baltic states to the responsive, yet comparatively relaxed attitude of Finland.

Yet we have no reason to be complacent. We should not take the stability of our institutions, the fairness of our markets, or the inclusiveness of our social contract for granted. Our deep integration with our European and Western neighbors means that to no little degree their vulnerabilities are our vulnerabilities too. In particular, we need to listen to our citizens more carefully. The double-digit votes for the AfD, and the amount of fear and hate that is articulated on German social media websites without a hint of a Russian accent should teach us that there are many Germans who feel left out or left behind—by disconnected elites, by institutions, by parties, by economic progress, or simply by globalization. Reunification in 1990 created many winners, but alienated many others. The global financial crisis, the arrival of a record number of refugees, and not least Germany's new leadership role have left many citizens worried and overwhelmed. Indeed, the successes of Russian interference—such as they are—are a measure of our failures.

12.   What could happen? Scenarios, responses—and the importance of America

At this point, it is impossible to predict with any confidence what form Russian interference in the September 24 elections could take. A major terrorist attack or a return of the refugee crisis would no doubt lend itself to propagandistic exploitation. Further DDOS attacks of the kind perpetrated on the Bundestag are also conceivable, as are leaks from the 2015 hack. Yet it is just as likely that a visible Russian attempt to use such events to further its own narratives would have entirely the opposite effect—as has been seen already. So, rather than a "big splash" incident, interference might just as well take the form of ongoing careful probing and testing of our vulnerabilities, combined with a continuous slow drip of toxic disinformation.

That means Germany will have to remain vigilant, but also flexible and relaxed. It will have to continue to work on its resilience, but not over-dramatize the scope, intent or coherence of the Russian threat. In fact, to do so would be to walk into the main psychological trap of Kremlin propaganda: to see the threat as larger than it actually is. (Russia is by no means the only country meddling in the German political space: Turkey, Iran, and above all China are similarly active.) And while some aspects of the threats emanating from Russia are military and require a military response, it would be a mistake to frame all acts of Russian interference as warfare, and react accordingly. In a democracy, the battle of ideas should and can take place in the political marketplace.

Still, it is beyond question that Germany and all of Europe are experiencing a phase of historic volatility and risk, in which the threat of Russian interference is only one of many. In such times, friends and allies matter more than ever. The prospect of Brexit looks set to deprive the EU of one of its most capable members.

That makes our relationship with America all the more important. We understand that Europe needs to do more for its own defense, and take some of the burden of the transatlantic security relationship off the United States; we have already taken steps towards this goal. But the alliance as such—our political, economic, military, and intelligence partnership—is crucial for the preservation of the European project. An America that feels ambiguous about the value of this alliance could be perceived in the Kremlin as the ultimate encouragement.

Endnotes

[1] Dana Priest and Michael Birnbaum, "Europe has been working to expose Russian meddling for years," *Washington Post*, June 26, 2017.

[2] Stefan Meister, "Germany: interdependence as vulnerability," in Atlantic Council, "The Kremlin's Trojan Horses," November 2016, page 12.

[3] Bundesministerium des Inneren/German Interior Ministry, Verfassungsschutzbericht 2015, page 256-7.

[4] Deutsche Welle, "Chancellor Merkel faces President Putin in tense Sochi press conference," May 2, 2017.

[5] BBC, "German spy chief Kahl warns of election disruption," November 29, 2016.

[6] Andrea Shalal, "Germany challenges Russia over alleged cyberattacks," *Reuters*, May 4, 2017.

[7] Bundesministerium des Inneren/German Interior Ministry, Verfassungsschutzbericht 2015, page 254.

[8] See, e.g. Stefan Meister and Jana Puglierin, "Perception and Exploitation: Russia' non-military influence in Europe," DGAP Kompakt No. 10, October 2015.

[9] Berthold Kohler and Eckhart Lohse, "Ich bin gut angekommen," interview with German president Frank Walter Steinmeier, *Frankfurter Allgemeine Zeitung*, June 16, 2017.

[10] ZEIT Online, "Bundestagswahl nicht durch Hacker in Gefahr," January 1, 2017.

[11] Ben Nimmo, "The Kremlin's Amplifiers in Germany," Digital Forensic Research Lab, June 22, 2017.

[12] Patrick Beuth, Marc Brost, Peter Dausend, Steffen Dobbert, Götz Hamann, "War Without Blood," ZEIT Online, February 28, 2017.

[13] According to Nimmo (ibid.), NewsFront has 2,254 followers, Sputnik Deutsch has 14,700, and RT Deutsch 29,200—compared to the national press agency Deutsche Presse Agentur (dpa) with 258,000 or ZEIT Online with 1,890,000. He points out that they do better on Facebook: RT Deutsch has 270,000 followers, Sputnik Deutschland has 181,000, and NewsFront Deutsch has 11,000—but still lag behind major established outlets like Die Welt (868,000) or ZEIT Online (773,000).

[14] The *Russlanddeutsche* (Russian-Germans) are descendants of German settlers who moved to Russia and modern Kazakhstan in the 18th century, preserving their original language and cultural memories; following the dissolution of the Soviet Union, an estimated two million returned to united Germany. A 2016 study by the Boris Nemtsov Foundation for Freedom shows that Russian state television in particular remains an important source of information; see http://nemtsovfund.org/en/2016/11/boris-nemtsov-foundation-s-survey-russian-speaking-germans/.

[15] Bundesamt für Flüchtlinge und Migration, "(Spät-) Aussiedler in Deutschland," December 3, 2013, page 28.

[16] Patrick Beuth, Marc Brost, Peter Dausend, Steffen Dobbert, Götz Hamann, "War Without Blood," ZEIT Online, February 28, 2017.

[17] Patrick Beuth, Kai Biermann, Martin Klingst, and Holger Stark, "Merkel and the Fancy Bear," ZEIT Online, May 12, 2017. So far, none of the documents siphoned off in the Bundestag attack have found their way into the public domain or onto a Wikileaks site; but it is possible that the purpose of the attack was espionage rather than the procurement of compromising materials (*kompromat*). For an excellent analysis of the issues, see the Transatlantic Cyber Forum's "Cyber Operations: Defending Political IT Infrastructures," to be published by Stiftung Neue Verantwortung this week.

[18] Bundesministerium des Inneren/German Interior Ministry, Verfassungsschutzbericht 2015, page 254-255.

[19] Mark Galeotti, "The 'Trump Dossier' or How Russia Helped America Break Itself," *Tablet Magazine*, June 13, 2017.

[20] Esther King, "Russian Hackers Targeting Germany: Intelligence Chief," *Politico*, November 29, 2016.

[21] Mark Galeotti, "The 'Trump Dossier' or How Russia Helped America Break Itself," *Tablet Magazine*, June 13, 2017.

[22] Emnid, "Sonntagsfrage" (What if the national elections were next Sunday), June 24, 2017.

[23] Statistisches Bundesamt (DESTATIS), "Foreign trade: Ranking of Germany's trading partners in foreign trade," June 21, 2017, page 2.

[24] Clint Watts and Andrew Weisburd, "How Russia wins an election," *Politico Magazine*, December 13, 2016.

[25] Thorsten Benner and Mirko Hohmann have criticized this approach as a privatization of the enforcement of the legal limits of free speech, "Internet companies can't be judges of free speech," *Politico*, April 18, 2017.

[26] Tanjev Schultz, Nickolaus Kackob, Marc Ziegele, Oliver Quiring, and Christian Schemer, „Erosion des Vertrauens zwischen Medien und Publikum?," Media Perspektiven 5/2017, page 246.

Chairman BURR. Thank you, Doctor, and thank you, all of our witnesses.

A reminder that we will recognize members by seniority for up to five minutes. The Chair recognizes himself.

Two questions to all of you. They are yes and no, yes or no. Do you have any doubt that Russian interference is driven by Putin himself?

Start with you, Ambassador Burns.

Ambassador BURNS. No doubt about it.

Chairman BURR. Ambassador.

Ambassador GARCEVIC. The same answer. No doubt.

Mr. SARTS. No doubt.

Dr. STELZENMUELLER. None.

Chairman BURR. Any doubt that Russian interference is or has happened in the U.S. and European elections?

Ambassador BURNS. It has happened systematically.

Ambassador GARCEVIC. It happened, it happens, and it is going to happen.

Mr. SARTS. It has happened.

Dr. STELZENMUELLER. A little difficult to vary on this, but yes.

Chairman BURR. Ambassador Garcevic, what would have happened in Montenegro had Russia succeeded in the parliamentary elections?

Ambassador GARCEVIC. You can imagine, I would say, first what could have happened is that The democratic front would withdraw sanctions which were imposed by my country on Russia, because my country was among the few in the region to impose sanctions immediately after they were imposed by the E.U. in order to show, to demonstrate, full alliance with the E.U. Common Foreign and Security Policy. That could be the first immediate step to be taken.

The second, in terms of far-reaching goals, they would turn the direction of the country from Western-leaning to Eastern-leaning, which means that I can imagine that in years from now Montenegro would become a satellite of Russia in the Balkans.

Chairman BURR. Mr. Sarts, was there any evidence of Russian involvement in the U.K. most recent elections?

Mr. SARTS. Of course, both RT and Sputnik made their effort to have an effect on the election. But I would not say—I would not say that there has been a significant pattern of Russian involvement in the U.K. election that we have seen. I would also argue that it is always—we have a pattern that Russia requires time to construct elaborate operations to attack the election systems. So where there's very little preparatory time for enhancing the networks, activating the networks, and planning for these things, they are not really efficient.

Chairman BURR. I took from your testimony that media outlets are directed in many cases by Russian government as to how they cover elections, what they say or don't say about candidates. So just the fact that maybe RT and Sputnik had a narrative that was different in Britain than maybe the mainstream press, that would be a sign of Russia trying to influence the outcome, would it not?

Mr. SARTS. I have no direct evidence to say that the particular narratives as we see in these outlets during the election period in the U.K. would have been directly directed from Kremlin, although there is a regular monthly meeting between all the key editors of media in Russia with the Kremlin officials, where reportedly they coordinate the messaging.

Chairman BURR. So it's not a news outlet as we would define in the United States, independent?

Mr. SARTS. No.

Chairman BURR. If I understood your testimony, again, I think there was a suggestion that America's social media platforms knew that they were part of a coordinated attack, especially as it related to France. Did I hear you correctly?

Mr. SARTS. The media platforms have the data to see where the information originates, and I know they've been also assisting the French media to make sure that within these platforms the information that these consortiums find as factually correct have the preeminence.

Chairman BURR. Media outlets have the ability to understand whether a bot has been used to make it look like there's tremendous public support for an issue versus real public support. Is that an accurate statement?

Mr. SARTS. Well, yes, it is. Actually it is more than just the media themselves. There is increased number of research—and also we are about to publish a regular report on robotic networks and social media—that these robotic systems are pushing the specific narratives. What we've seen is the same robotic networks working on the Dutch elections, pushing the RT–Sputnik-Russian narrative, or for that matter also in a French election pushing the Le Pen narrative, or country, also pushing all the fake stories about Emmanuel Macron.

Chairman BURR. Last question. Nick Burns, what should the U.S. response be? And should that response to election integrity and intrusion by the Russians be coordinated with our European partners?

Ambassador BURNS. I think it should. I think there are three things we can do, Mr. Chairman. And I hope the Administration is beginning to do some of this. First is our intelligence agencies have to be linked up to understand the threat as it's happening.

Second, if laws are being broken in both Europe and the United States, our judicial authorities ought to be working together to prosecute people and put them behind bars.

And third—and this will probably happen through Secretary Tillerson and others and our ambassadors overseas—in the response—and you saw this brilliant response by the Macron campaign to push back—we can be lashed up with the Europeans in a response to an attack, whether it's in Europe or the United States. We're in the same NATO alliance, all the countries represented here today are. It's a political alliance as well as a military alliance. We ought to be working together.

And finally, I think that the Senate is on the right track with your sanctions bill. It's a tough bill. I know it's caused some controversy in some countries in Europe. But frankly, American companies—European companies shouldn't have advantages to sell into the Russian market that American companies do not have. And I think your bill makes that point.

Chairman BURR. Thank you, Ambassador.

53

Vice Chairman.

Vice Chairman WARNER. Thank you, Mr. Chairman.

Let me again thank all the witnesses for their testimony, and thank you again for your unanimous agreement on the nature of the Russian threat and the attacks that were created here in the United States.

I want to go back. In our March public hearing, one of our witnesses, Clint Watts, testified that then-candidate Trump, quote, "used Russian active measures at times against his opponents," end of quote. He cited then-candidate Trump's coordination or use in calling out WikiLeaks. We saw candidate Trump continue to use terms like the elections being "rigged," the same type of terms that were used by the Kremlin in their propaganda efforts.

Do you agree with what Mr. Watts drew as a conclusion, that, at least inadvertently, candidate Trump was actually advancing the goals of the Russian propaganda efforts? I'd like to hear any of your comments on that, starting with you, Ambassador Burns.

Ambassador BURNS. Senator, just two quick points. First, I don't have any independent knowledge about the Trump campaign working with——

Vice Chairman WARNER. I'm not asking that. I'm just asking whether his comments about elections being rigged, calling on WikiLeaks—it appeared, and Mr. Watts drew the conclusion, that, at least inadvertently, it seemed that then-candidate Trump was actually aligned with some of what Russia's propaganda efforts were trying to sow the same kind of chaos and questioning of our democratic processes.

Ambassador BURNS. Right. I thought it was just important to say I don't have information. But when candidate Trump did encourage the Russian government to find more of Secretary Clinton's e-mails, I thought that was an irresponsible statement.

Vice Chairman WARNER. Anybody else want to comment?

[No response.]

You're taking a safe diplomatic effort, all of you. I appreciate that.

I imagine I will get the same response, because I again share very much, Ambassador Burns, your comments earlier that the lack of interest shown by the President of even acknowledging this threat or taking this threat—urging his Administration to take this threat seriously and lay out a coordinated whole-of-government approach to what will be a threat in 2017, 2018. I would argue that Putin and his cronies had a pretty darn good rate of return on the number of rubles invested in their activities to kind of take on our election system.

Mr. Sarts, one of the questions—I want to go back to commend you for your good work on the 18 reports that you've done on the robot trolling and how the Russians are using technology tools to exponentially increase the power of their fake news.

You've said—you've cited reports that at least 8 percent of Twitter accounts are actually bot accounts and thereby do not represent an actual person. Facebook—I was out recently with Facebook, and they pointed out the fact that in the French elections they took down about 30,000 fake accounts right before the election. I commend them because right after the American election Facebook acted like they had no responsibility for policing fake news. I think they've moved into a more responsible position.

But I'd love to hear from all of you what role you feel these platform companies that control so much information—Google, Facebook, Twitter, et al.—have in this new world. And again, we'll go down the list, starting with you, Ambassador Burns.

Ambassador BURNS. Senator, very briefly, I had the opportunity to be at Stanford for 5 months last year; met a lot of these people who work in this space. And I was impressed by the number of people—take YouTube for example—that they now dedicate to try to filter out hate speech. And that's commendable.

If that's the case, there ought to be an ongoing dialogue between the U.S. Government, our national security agencies, and these companies to try to filter out Russian propaganda. It's a direct assault on our country.

I was impressed by Mr. Sarts' testimony. I thought it was quite convincing that there has to be an integration of the technology companies and our government on this issue.

Vice Chairman WARNER. I concur. I'd love to hear the rest of your comments, please.

Mr. SARTS. Well, first, I also just came yesterday back from Silicon Valley, where we talked with a lot of these companies on these issues. First, there's a growing market, black market, for robotics in social media. Some of it is rather innocent, but much of that is of some kind of criminal activity. And that is going to be a growing concern for people in a digital environment to actually understand that they're really interacting with a human being, instead of large numbers of robots supported by artificial intelligence.

To counter that, the companies that have these platforms are one of the key players. I was heartened by the discussion back there. They are taking it seriously, probably slightly too late. But there are—most of these big companies are investing in and thinking about how they can be an active supporter of a democratic process, not a disrupter.

And secondly, there is a growing number of the technology research on the subject that we can rely on. And as Ambassador Burns said, and I've said in my initial statement, that is a must that we work together. If we don't, we will not succeed in the digital environment.

Vice Chairman WARNER. Have seen any cooperation in Germany? My time is expired.

Dr. STELZENMUELLER. Yes, sir. German politicians and policymakers have made trips to Silicon Valley to talk to the big media companies and tech companies like Google, Facebook and Twitter. I've been told the initial conversations were less than, shall we say, less than cooperative. There seemed to be no inclination to self-police and there also was no inclination to help. That has significantly changed, I gather.

Now, the German justice minister has just put out a draft of a law called the Netzwerkdurchsetzungsgesetz—and we use these long words to annoy our allies. But, basically, it's a draft law to help in enforcing hate speech rules in Germany, which are quite strong, obviously, with roots in our history.

I as a trained constitutional lawyer and other critics of this law, have mixed feelings about this. I would like the political marketplace to regulate itself. But if significant actors, very powerful actors that have control over algorithms that can really shape the marketplace without citizens even noticing if they refuse to self-police, I believe such laws become necessary. I think this has to be an ongoing conversation between business, citizens and the state, to decide where responsibility for regulation properly lies.

Chairman BURR. Senator Risch.

Senator RISCH. Thank you.

Ambassador Burns, you know, we're pretty used to dealing with hyperbole in this Committee with the kind of things that we hear, and I want to talk to you for a minute about your statement that Russia is the most dangerous adversary that we have. With all due respect, if you sat on this Committee I'm not sure you'd reach that conclusion.

I think there's a lot of us, with what we hear about what's going on in North Korea and some of our other adversaries, that Russia certainly is a dangerous adversary, but when you have someone running a country like Kim Jong Un and with what we know about what he's probably going to do if his administration is threatened, I've got to tell you that you might be slightly off mark when you say that that Russia's the most dangerous adversary that we face.

But don't take that as a criticism that I think that Russia is not a dangerous adversary. I would just caution that it falls in a group of countries, and there's others that are more dangerous.

You were critical of or are critical of President Trump and what he's thinking right now. You would agree with me that the Russians have taken no active measures in an election while Donald Trump has been President? Is that a fair statement?

Ambassador BURNS. Senator, thank you. May I just say in response to your first comment, if you would allow it?

Senator RISCH. Please.

Ambassador BURNS. I agree with everything you said about North Korea, but Russia can do greater damage to us from a nuclear weapons perspective and certainly in trying to draw a new dividing line in Europe. So it's a respectful disagreement.

Senator RISCH. I appreciate that and let me ask you this. Do you think it's more likely that that would come—assuming that North Korea had nuclear weapons that they could deliver, is it more likely that it would come from Russia or from North Korea?

Ambassador BURNS. Well, I think the problem—the threat from Russia is multifaceted. It's not just from nuclear weapons. It's also about dividing Europe.

Senator RISCH. No question about that.

Ambassador BURNS. So I think they are both a problem——

Senator RISCH. I agree with that.

Ambassador BURNS [continuing]. A big problem for the United States. I just made the statement—I was echoing General Dunford, when he was confirmed.

Senator RISCH. Back to my last question, you would agree with me that the Russians have taken no active measures in an American election while Donald Trump has been President? Is that a fair statement?

Ambassador BURNS. Well, I think it might—I actually don't know. I don't know what have——

Senator RISCH. Have we had any elections since he's been President?

Ambassador BURNS. Yes, we've had Congressional elections.

Senator RISCH. And you think that the Russians have taken some active measures in those elections?

Ambassador BURNS. I don't know the answer to that question.

Senator RISCH. We do know that the Russians took active measures in the last presidential election?

Ambassador BURNS. Well, I think the intelligence communities of the United States are confirmed on that, yes.

Senator RISCH. I think we're all in agreement with that. That—and who was President of the United States when that occurred?

Ambassador BURNS. That was President Obama, as you know.

Senator RISCH. And you know he was aware that this was going on?

Ambassador BURNS. Yes.

Senator RISCH. Indeed, he's admitted that he talked to Mr. Putin about that, is that correct?

Ambassador BURNS. So you heard my testimony about President Obama. I have great respect for President Obama. This was a difficult decision.

Senator RISCH. I hear that.

Ambassador BURNS. I think that President Obama, with the benefit of hindsight, should have acted more resolutely, quickly, to be transparent with the American people. But he did take action. And what disturbs me about President Trump is that he's not investigating, has taken no action.

Senator RISCH. Got that. But I'm talking about somebody that could have done something about this while it was going on. You're aware that President Obama talked to Mr. Putin about that, are you not, in the summer of 2016?

Ambassador BURNS. That's what the news reports say. I also know that the Obama Administration briefed the eight senior members of Congress early on, that there were public statements made by Jeh Johnson, I think on October 7th. So they did take action. It's not as if the Obama Administration just was silent on this issue.

Senator RISCH. And indeed, when Mr.—or when President Obama told Mr. Putin that we knew that they were taking active measures, that was indeed a classified—that was classified information, was it not?

Ambassador BURNS. Well, you know, I think if you're the President of United States and you're trying to deliver a stiff diplomatic mission, you're well within your rights to tell Putin what you think he may be doing.

Senator RISCH. I couldn't agree with you more.

Ambassador BURNS. In fact, that's the object of the conversation.

Senator RISCH. Couldn't agree with you more. And that's actually the purpose of classified information. It's no good if you collect it and don't use it. Fair statement?

Ambassador BURNS. Well, not always. Sometimes you don't want that information ever to see the light of day.

Senator RISCH. What else should—what else should President Obama have done?

Ambassador BURNS. You know—and this is Monday morning quarterbacking by me

Senator RISCH. I understand that.

Ambassador BURNS. And I appreciate the fact that he finally did take action on the sanctions. I think if you go back and look at it, the American people in my judgment deserved to know what was happening clearly. You have to ring the village bell. And we should have had a more immediate response that was painful to the Russians, whether that was immediate sanctions or some type of offensive action that we could have taken by covert means against them. And so I think, there are a variety of options. I wasn't there, so I don't want to micromanage this.

Senator RISCH. I appreciate that.

Ambassador BURNS. But I do think that he could have done more. But my testimony clearly shows that President Trump has taken no action whatsoever and I think that's irresponsible.

Senator RISCH. Got that. But the description you gave, you would agree with me that the Obama Administration did not take significantly—the significant action that was needed, including informing the American people, which would have gone a long ways to countering what the Russians did? Fair statement?

Ambassador BURNS. Well, I think that the Obama Administration should have taken greater action, but the more pertinent question today is what our current President is not doing, and that has implications for Europe and they're very negative.

Senator RISCH. To you it's the more pertinent. To me, what's more pertinent is what should have been done by the commander-in-chief who was in charge at that time.

My time is up. Thank you, Mr. Chairman.

Chairman BURR. Senator Feinstein.

Senator FEINSTEIN. Thanks very much, Mr. Chairman.

Many have said this is actually the crime of the century. If you think about it, it is. If you think about the fact that it's conducted by intelligence agencies, we know Russian intelligence to be relentless and ruthless, and it all happened, and it contributed toward the defeat of an American presidential candidate, who happened to be the first woman running for that office. Well, that's not true, but in a very serious, ineluctable way it is. They targeted 21 states. They went into 21 states.

I've been sitting here, Nick, listening to you, listening to your colleagues. I have great respect for you. My own view is that if in fact this is the crime of the century, if in fact it's going to lead to other crimes being committed in the future, that we together have a responsibility to hit back. The question comes, are sanctions really the effective way to do it or do we do it in the cyber world?

But I don't think that we can sit here and see the amount of destruction that has been done, the defeat of a candidate, the intrusion into 21 State systems, the continuation even now with spear phishing, what's happening in Europe, and, you know, the Iron Bear is on a march.

How do you stop that? And we have had certain abilities discussed of how to develop a hit-back. And it's hard for me to believe that—sanctions make them angry, but sanctions don't really do anything. There is a downside to a cyber war. On the other hand, the United States of America cannot see the critical infrastructure of an American democratic election destroyed by Russia.

What—I'd be very interested if anyone would be prepared to talk about what Europe and America could do together to plan, to prepare, and to hit back.

Ambassador BURNS. Senator, I'd just say briefly, our sanctions have to be aligned. They'll be much stronger if we actually work together with the Europeans to align what they do in sanctions with us, number one.

Number two, it's my impression we can do much more in the way of intelligence, but also in active work together to respond verbally to the propaganda.

But number three, I think you're right, and I so testified, that we have to think of other means. And we have capacity that if we wanted to use it, we could. And that has to be aligned with Europe.

Senator FEINSTEIN. Bear in mind, these aren't fringe people. These are two, at least two of the three intelligence services of Russia. That's a big deal. The President of Russia committed his intelligence services to hit our election system. Do we just, oh, well, maybe we shut off this sanction or that sanction? Maybe we think it's going to just go away? They show no signs of going away.

I've been on this Committee for a long time. I have never seen a time when, with full confidence, every single one of America's intelligence agencies have come together and say they have—they have full confidence that this was orchestrated by Putin and he used his intelligence services to do it.

Mr. SARTS. Well, if I may, I think the first thing that we have to do is cover our backs. And that is building the resilience. That was the things that we all three talk—four talked about.

Senator FEINSTEIN. Could you define "resilience"?

Mr. SARTS. Ability of the democratic process to withstand the attacks, overt or covert, to influence, with a malicious intent from outside, the societal choices within the election system, within the political process. And being able to, irrespective, of these——

Senator FEINSTEIN. With what acts, sir? We do stand in a— there's no question about that. But——

Mr. SARTS. Well, I can go through the things that I recommended: society being aware; cyber defense being on a high level; having been able to operationalize the information battlespace, and many of these.

Secondly, I wanted to say in fact, if you look at Russian documents, they believe we are attacking them, and I think they really believe that. So—which is, I think, a paradox.

What we have to really look for is that we're not attacked by Russians, we're attacked by Kremlin. And what we can do is actually help also people within Russia to recognize what is the actual realities. I think that is the most powerful weapon, the truth, the truth that Kremlin is hiding away from their own citizens. And that is I think the weapon that we have which is the most mighty.

Senator FEINSTEIN. My time is up. Thank you.

Chairman BURR. Senator Rubio.

Ambassador GARCEVIC. Excuse me. May I add a few words? I personally lived in a country which was under sanctions and I have my personal experience of being a citizen of a country and living a normal life in a country under sanctions. For sanctions to start working and to start bearing fruits, you need time. It took like nine years for Yugoslavia, which was smaller, in economic terms very smaller than Russia, to see sanctions working.

I can imagine that in the case of Russia, we have to endure. Perseverance is needed, and sanctions will start bearing fruits at certain point. So, I don't think that we should stop or rethink this strategy.

On top of it, someone mentioned, I think the Ambassador, mentioned importance of NATO, because NATO is not only military organization. NATO is security and political organization. Since it was formed in 1949, U.S. has seen NATO as a pillar of Euro-Atlantic bond. And the countries who are members of NATO are there because of a set of values that they share, which means that we have to keep ourselves together and strong through NATO, which includes a number of measures. Not only a deterrence, which is taking place right now in Europe, but also a number of other measures, because it's not only that Europe is under attack. Its values are under attack. Values are under attack, values of democracy, values of parliamentary democracy, value of liberal democracies are under attack.

Russia is backing those groups in Europe, leftist or rightist, those who challenge the very core values of liberal democracy, because those who challenge from within those democratic systems and would like to see those systems and values eroding.

So in power with some hard-core or hard power measures, we have to put emphasis also on soft power, because this is what Russia uses against democratic systems. I think democratic systems in soft-power are much better off than Russia and may offer more than Russia can offer to countries.

Chairman BURR. Doctor.

Dr. STELZENMUELLER. Madam Senator, I would like to add one small remark to what's already been said, and that is, if I may say as an ally and a citizen of your ally of over 60 years: Do no harm. Do not question the alliance. Do not question the alliance that is greatly in your strategic interest with Europe, but that is also in our interest. It is of existential importance for us. And an American government, a White House, that questions the validity of that alliance, that questions the validity of the Article 5 mutual defense commitment, does more to undermine our security and our safety than many things that the Kremlin does.

We are all vibrant Western democracies. That's not to say we don't have flaws and vulnerabilities. And we should not only address those, but we I think as Western democracies can address them together. We can look at them together.

And I would add only one thing. Sanctions do work, perhaps even more as a political statement of cohesion and will, and as such they have had a tremendous impact on Russia. They have left a deep impression on the Kremlin. They have also done some economic damage, but they have above all been an expression of Europe's and America's will to stand together against the threat toward

Ukraine and its neighbors and the threat against the European project and American interests there. So they do work.

Thank you.

Chairman BURR. Senator Rubio.

Senator RUBIO. Thank you.

Thank you all for being here.

My hope is that this Committee's work will produce a document that doesn't simply detail what happened, but how they did it, so that we can prevent—so that we can take steps, preventive steps to address this in the future, because I don't believe it's going away any time soon, for one simple reason: It worked.

And I think we're all—a lot of people are focused on a particular electoral outcome. I think the broader design was to sow instability, chaos, division in a country that already had great political division. I don't think anybody can doubt that that's the case.

I mean, just the sheer amount of time and energy that's been spent by this Committee, this Congress, the press and everybody else on this issue of Russia alone must be deeply gratifying to the people who authorized these measures. And the way it's exacerbated our ability to get work done on a number of other things has been deeply impactful.

And so I really, truly hope that as we do our work we will learn what are the best ways to confront it, within the confines of the following. We have a First Amendment. So I understand that places like France are able to block out. You know, when the stuff came out about Macron they had a blackout at the end period, and so a lot of that was not widely reported.

I don't mean this in a—I'm not attacking the media. I'm just saying, one of the most powerful unwitting agents of Russian influence was the mainstream media, that when these e-mails were being leaked from WikiLeaks there was a lot of focus on what was in the gossipy aspects of it and not so much the origins of what it was all about.

And, because it's a—we have the First Amendment in this country, and so the people who did this understood that certain information would get widespread coverage. I'm not advocating censorship. I'm telling you, that is what they'll use against us. So, we have that different from what they have in Europe and the like.

I want to know, what has worked? Has anyone successfully confronted this threat and proven to us things you can do to alleviate the sting of these efforts? I point to an article in "The New York Times" by several authors on May 9th of 2017. It talks about steps taken by Macron's campaign, including creating dozens of false e-mail accounts, complete with phony documents, to confuse the attackers.

I'm curious, Ambassador Garcevic, about the efforts in Montenegro, a small country that has far closer historical, cultural, and religious ties to Russia, and where Russian state media and propaganda run rampant. They were unable to dissuade the people there from electing a pro-NATO government. What works? Because—has anyone begun to figure this out? Because we need to do it.

Mr. SARTS. Well, first, what works is people don't like to be manipulated, and when they know somebody's out there for them to change their mind and get under their skin they become more cautious. That's the first thing. And we've seen in a number of countries where the public becomes aware, it's much harder, like instantly, to get the effect the Russians are trying to achieve.

Secondly, it is I think very important in these, especially misinformation. The Marcon case, you know it is going to happen; you do a contingency plan. And I would say your contingency is not that they're not going to break in. There's always a way through the human fault you can get into the systems.

You actually, as they did, you do a trap. You do a trap. That's another thing that has clearly worked. And that takes also the knowledge, preparation, and acceptance that it is happening.

And thirdly, in the fake news cycles we see it is always that the fake news comes in first, creates emotion and gets wider. If you are able to get into that cycle first, you are limiting the effect, if not taking it away as such. And we've seen cases in Lithuania where the fake stories about German soldiers raping a teenage girl were trying to circulate, where the government and media actually made sure the first news somebody ever sees was: There is the fake news news that this and this. And they, those government and the media worked their part, and that never got traction.

So there are quite a number of good, successful, tactical and strategic examples that one can look at.

Ambassador GARCEVIC. If I may add two things. What was Russia's goal? What is Russia's goal in the region? It goes beyond Montenegro. Russia's goal is to prevent the expansion of NATO and the E.U. It's not only about Montenegro. It's about other countries that are wavering or that are not fully on either side.

You know, if Montenegro is considered or can be considered now as a lost case for Russia, others are not lost case yet. And Russia is trying to, by making example in Montenegro, is trying to send a signal to others: what we are willing to do or what we can do if you even dare to go the same way. This is really from a strategical point of view, it comes through the Balkans, this corner of Europe, important for Russia.

But it comes to how media campaign was carried out in Montenegro also speaks that Russia has really a diversified approach. And it adopted its approach toward Montenegro how to reach out to people in Montenegro, and not only Montenegro, but in the region.

Montenegro, first of all, we are not used to watching Russian TV. We are not used to reading Russian newspapers in Russian. We are not like people in Ukraine, for example. We don't have Russian communities living in Montenegro. So they therefore decided to open, to establish, a number of offices of Russian media in the region that would broadcast news in all local language, and then to use local networks to republish those news. First fabricate news, make either fake or false news, then those news will be broadcasted or republished further by local news. Then people will trust local news or local media, if not Russian media. After some time Sputnik and Russia Today have become the most popular among local population.

And finally, because of cultural and historical and religious closeness between two nations, they really effectively use church and state. My society is in principle a traditional society and people trust priests and trust church. And since we are also Orthodox population, as Russians are, so they use church to propagate Orthodox style of life or Eastern Orthodox style of life and to present to the people, to citizens of my country, that it's about identity and it's about cultural roots and it's about dignity; and that Eastern Christianity is fundamentally different than Western world. And if we join NATO or the E.U., at the end of the day we're going to lose our identity, and it's about dignity.

So, this is how effectively Russia uses different channels, different mechanisms, in order to reach our people and to send message which will be, how to say, in order to earn the hearts of people they would like to have on their side.

Chairman BURR. Senator Wyden.

Senator WYDEN. Thank you.

And thank the four of you. This has been a very valuable panel.

Here in our inquiry, I've focused on what I called the follow-the-money issues, and concerns about Moscow's funding of pro-Russia political parties and groups in Europe, of course, is not new. Two years ago, the Committee directed the National Intelligence Office to submit an intelligence assessment on this issue. What is different now is we are looking at this attack on European democracies to help us understand what has happened to our democracy.

So, Director Sarts, I want to start with you because you have studied Moscow's financing of pro-Russian political figures. And let me just kind of see if we can go through a few questions here. Have you been able to determine if Vladimir Putin employs particular strategies to develop relationships and curry favor with political figures in Europe? And if so, what would those strategies be?

Mr. SARTS. First, there are two strategies to incite different political actors across Europe into cooperating with Russia. First is financial incentives. It can work both through the opening of business opportunities vis-á-vis Kremlin-controlled companies, or it can work also through a number of funds controlled by Kremlin that send in further the money to different Russia-controlled NGOs, and then, therefore, further on, disseminating the financial means to incite people into cooperating.

The other venue is nonfinancial, which is giving the Russian information power as the backdrop to whoever's message they're trying to promote and whose political point of view they are trying to use for whatever their strategy——

Senator WYDEN. Does President Putin make the decision himself to support political figures in Europe, based again on what you know?

Mr. SARTS. Well, we as a center look explicitly at the open source. So I would not be able on my available information to make that conclusion.

Senator WYDEN. Does Russian assistance to its allies in Europe involve helping political parties, individual political figures, associates of individual political figures, or all of these different approaches?

Mr. SARTS. They do.

Senator WYDEN. They use all of the above.

And is there any information available on what mechanisms Putin prefers to provide financial assistance to political figures in Europe?

Mr. SARTS. In an open space, there have been a number of reports from the European intelligence agencies sketching out without great detail some of these practices. But of course, there is much more which is not within the open public space that is known on these activities.

Senator WYDEN. And one last one for you, Director Sarts. Your statement referred to Russian cyber-attacks, including the 2015 Russian hack of the German Bundestag. Last week, the U.K. Parliament came under what British authorities called a sustained and determined attack on all parliamentary user accounts, although the source of the attack has not been identified.

The reason I ask is my understanding with respect to these issues is every attack is going to be different. Every attack is going to be different because once you've engaged in one particular strategy, you've got people preparing for that and they move on to the next. What's your advice to us, based on your analysis in Europe, for how we deal with this extraordinarily important issue of developing a cyber-attack strategy, a preventive cyber-attack strategy?

Mr. SARTS. Well, first, I think you give too much credit to the Kremlin operations. In fact, what our research says, much of the tool set remains the same. There is a variation and there is an experimentation, but it is not more than the 20 percent of the overall activity.

The generic advice is that we have to think slightly differently about what the cyber-attack is. We typically think of it as a venue to get into the infrastructure and get the data. But I would argue that we have to think of two parameters: of course technical as very important; but at the end of the day, the purpose of the attack to get into the minds. And we have to actually, when employing our own countering strategies, focus both on technical as well as in the cognitive aspects of the defense.

Senator WYDEN. My time is up. I'm glad you think that the Russians are less clever than cyber-attackers elsewhere. I have reservations about that.

I just want to make one last point. I know my time is up, Mr. Chairman.

Ambassador Burns, I'm a fan of yours, and I just heard one word that concerned me with respect to the relationship of government and the technology companies. I think, and probably you didn't really really mean it—you talked about integrating the companies and the government. I think what you were meaning was better communication between the government and the companies, and I just wanted to make that point.

Thank you, Mr. Chairman.

Oh, if you would like to respond.

Ambassador BURNS. Very quickly. Thank you. I meant that there should be communication, not that there be formally integrative efforts. Thank you.

Senator WYDEN. I understand.

Chairman BURR. Senator Collins.

Senator COLLINS. Ambassador Burns, it's good to see you. Thank you for joining this panel this morning.

I'm struck as I listen to the testimony of all the witnesses that the approach that was used in Montenegro, in France, in Germany has been much more proactive. It's bolder. It exposes the falsehoods that are out there. And it is a far more visible effort.

Ambassador, you were somewhat critical of President Obama, and I would be even more critical of his response. And I would call it behind the scenes, ineffective, and tardy. It wasn't really until after the election that sanctions were imposed and that the January 6th, 2017, report on the extensiveness and the scope of Russian interference in our elections was released by the intelligence community.

So there seems to me to be a big difference in the approach that's taken by our allies and the approach that was taken by President Obama. And as you pointed out rightly, President Trump's Administration does not seem to have any strategy to deal with this going forward at this point.

But then I hear about the efforts taken in France, for example, where there was a coordinated effort among government, the media, the campaigns, and even the technology companies. And there's one headline that says "French newsrooms unite to fight election misinformation." I just can't even imagine a headline in the United States saying "American newsrooms unite to fight election misinformation."

So are our systems so different that, while we can learn from our allies much more successful efforts to counter Russian active measures, is that even possible in our country, given the very different role of the media here? And I'm asking Ambassador Burns that question.

Ambassador BURNS. Thank you, Senator. You know, I think we're learning the lessons as we go along. And I think Director Comey was right when the Committee asked him about this, that he thinks that the next target in our country could be either party. And I applaud the bipartisan effort to try to learn the lessons.

The Europeans have learned lessons from what went wrong in our election. And what seems to have worked well in the Macron campaign is speed and decisive action and transparency so that actually all the French people were made aware of the threat. And they have a right to that information.

That was the basis of my criticism. And I just want to say this. I have tremendous respect for President Obama. This is Monday morning quarterback by somebody who is not in the government, but you're asked to testify and I think this is one of the lessons that we have to learn from the Europeans, how they've done.

And what's missing, it seems, is formal integration of effort by the governments of Canada, the United States and Europe. That's a step that the Trump Administration could decide to take, which would be very helpful both in analysis and also in action.

Senator COLLINS. I completely agree with you that visibility and transparency are absolutely critical, and that is an important lesson from what happened last fall.

Ambassador Garcevic, I want to ask you about Montenegro because the State of Maine has a special relationship with Montenegro, and I can see by your smile that you're aware of that. We're part of the State Partnership Program and our National Guard has members stationed in Montenegro to assist the military and we like to think we were helpful in getting you ready for your NATO accession, which I strongly supported.

But Montenegro is a really interesting example, because Russia was not able, despite a tremendous effort, to dissuade the people there from electing a pro-NATO government last October. So my question to you is this: Why were the Russian influence efforts unsuccessful in Montenegro, which is a small country that has far closer historical and cultural, religious ties to Russia, and where the Russian state media and propaganda are prevalent, even as their efforts appeared to be much more successful—that's probably an overstatement, but to have some success—in sowing the seeds of doubt and discord in the 2016 election in our country?

Ambassador GARCEVIC. That's very difficult to answer in a couple of minutes. Sometimes—yes, we are a small country. Russia is big. I would say that Russia looked down on us as just peanuts in the Balkans that they can put in order easily. But it turned out not to be the case. Sometimes we had simply luck when one of the computers of one of our people in the mission to NATO was hacked by Russia. Simply, we were lucky because another mission—I don't want to mention name—which had been under attack with the same virus, computer virus, helped us register—detect that virus even before it started working, you know? And then we turned to NATO and then, with the help of NATO people, we checked all computers, not only in the mission to NATO, but also in the Ministry of Foreign Affairs and Military Defense, and government offices, and so now that we were not affected.

Sometimes, as I said, we had luck. But in more broader terms, I would say that Russia didn't penetrate economically, though at the first glance, on the surface, many seeked out Montenegro to explain how Montenegro was packed with Russians living there and with Russian money pouring in for years. But actually, Russian investments in Montenegro were mostly investments in real estate. We are not dependent on energy. The Russians didn't invest in banking sector. There are no investments in any of our important industrial branches in Montenegro, so they couldn't simply sway us easily.

Even when we imposed sanctions on them, they didn't know how to react economically on us, so they turned to some political measures in order to show that they are angry because of it.

And then, I would say, government, though we were small, what we tried to do, particularly when it comes to cyber attacks, we are not capable to hit back, definitely, but we tried to build a partnership with our NATO partners and we seek help from them.

Then, at the end of the day, when it comes to cyber attacks, it's about a human factor. And then we tried to build up vigilance and, you know, government issuing warning signs to its agencies to be careful how to deal with sensitive information.

Senator COLLINS. Thank you.

Thank you, Mr. Chairman.

Chairman BURR. Senator Heinrich.

Senator HEINRICH. Ambassador Burns, you've talked a lot about the sanctions bill we passed here in the Senate. If Speaker Ryan and the House of Representatives doesn't take up that Russia sanctions bill, what kind of message do you think that that would send to Vladimir Putin?

Ambassador BURNS. I think a message of weakness, because the Senate by a huge margin has teed this up. It's the right thing to do to have a painful type of leverage against the Russians. And if it's diluted in the House and if the Trump Administration encourages the House to do that, which is what one hears, then I think the Russians are going to receive a mixed message here, not a stiff message, which they need to receive.

Senator HEINRICH. Do you think it will send—make him more or less likely to interfere in the 2018 and 2020 elections?

Ambassador BURNS. You know, I read the transcript of your hearing with Director Comey. He told you that he thinks it's going to continue.

Senator HEINRICH. Yes.

Ambassador BURNS. Until we have better defenses, until we've gone on the offense.

I think that President Trump should consider, maybe Secretary Tillerson should do this—exactly what President Obama did. Go to Putin directly, as President Obama did. It was after our election, as Senator Collins pointed out, and just say, there are going to be consequences, and spell them out. That's actually probably the most effective thing that the Trump Administration should do.

Senator HEINRICH. Should we take these kinds of cyberattacks and election manipulation as seriously as we would take a military action or an economic threat to our country?

Ambassador BURNS. Well, as you know, they're different. Obviously, a military action is immediate, consequential. You have to respond within hours.

I actually think this is—what they try to do systematically to the Dutch, the Montenegrins, the French, the Germans and the Americans is discredit democracy in the eyes of our citizens. I use the word "existential" in my testimony. I don't think it was hyperbole. I think it was the right word to use. So I think we need to meet squarely. And all of us have suggested a multitude of ways that we can do that.

Senator HEINRICH. I don't disagree. I think one of the challenges that you've mentioned is that the current President has been unwilling to respond or even acknowledge the validity of the Russian hostile actions in the election. I'm curious what that means for what we as members of the Senate can or should do to advance a conversation with our European allies about sanctions. And I would certainly like your opinion on that, but I would open it to the other members on the panel as well.

Ambassador BURNS. That conversation has to be held. Normally in this situation, as you know, the State Department and the White House would be talking to the Germans, the Austrians about the consequences of the Senate bill. I don't know if this happened this time. But we're in this phase—we've talked about the separation of powers for 200 years—where it's my own view that Congress needs to play the leading role because I perceive Congress to be tougher against Russia.

Senator HEINRICH. Nature abhors a vacuum.

Do any of you want to add to that? Dr. Stelzenmueller.

Dr. STELZENMUELLER. Of course. It's well known that German politicians, senior German politicians, the chancellor and the foreign minister, have protested the sanctions bill. And this is, of course, because German companies, and not just German companies, other Europeans as well, are invested in Nord Stream 2.

I'm not a big fan of this project, frankly. But I'm far more concerned about unilateral American sanctions that aren't discussed with the Europeans, that are just put out there and we have to deal with them. The fact of the matter is that we had actually for years been asking America to allow the export of American LNG to the European market, and that it had been Congress that was resisting this.

So I think the lesson of this experience is for us to, as allies, discuss what is in the interest of the alliance and where we can work together. And I think that would be of significant importance as a deterrent towards Russia.

Senator HEINRICH. While I have you, Doctor, when President Trump questioned the value, the relevance of NATO, whether we should even keep it as a structure, who do you think benefitted most from that?

Dr. STELZENMUELLER. Well, I've already said that. I think that that helps the Kremlin, and it's not great. I also don't think it's in America's self-interest to question that alliance because you have significant interests in Europe and in Europe's periphery, and the alliance with us Europeans helps you pursue those national self-interests.

Senator HEINRICH. I could not agree more.

Mr. Sarts, before my time runs out, you talked a little about how we should try to take the truth directly to the Russian people because of the filter that they receive so much of their information through. How can we cut out Vladimir Putin and speak directly to the Russian people?

Mr. SARTS. Well, I think it is very clear and evident that is the same environment, which is the digital one. And if one takes note of the recent protests in Russia against the corruption, it was very striking how young the crowd was. And it was also very clear that these people don't anymore get their world view from the TV. It's all about also social networks. And yes, that's the way you can get the truth back to them. And I'm sure Kremlin will try to put up new elements to block us. But I think that is an environment where we can get back to them.

Senator HEINRICH. I want to thank you all for your testimony today.

Chairman BURR. Senator Blunt.

Senator BLUNT. Thank you, Chairman.

Let's try a yes-no question first, just in the interest of time. You know, the Russian economy is failing, not nearly the country it could or should be. Does Putin benefit in Russia from getting credit for interfering with elections in our countries? Ambassador.

Ambassador BURNS. I think he does. I think it builds him up.

Ambassador GARCEVIC. Yes, politically he does.

Mr. SARTS. It is one significant part for his domestic policy to benefit from it.

Dr. STELZENMUELLER. Sorry, I can't do a yes or no. I'd say it's both. In the short term, he benefits. In the long term, he loses and Russia loses.

Senator BLUNT. But the short-term benefit is?

Dr. STELZENMUELLER. The short-term benefit is it validates the narrative that we're all just as bad as Russia and, frankly, Russians are better off living in Russia because their life at least is stable.

The reality is that a lot of Kremlin interference has backfired and backfired visibly, and we've been learning from that. And it has taught us to review our complacencies. It's taught us to defend our democracies. That's a good thing. But we also are up against a significant enemy and one that has a lot of energy and patience.

Senator BLUNT. And in terms of—I was going to ask what we should do about these channels of miscommunication like in our country Sputnik and RT. Starting with you, Dr. Stelzenmueller: What have you—what, if anything, have you done to try to respond or immediately contradict information coming in? I mean, you're much closer to this than we are, but it's no harder to keep out here than it is there.

Dr. STELZENMUELLER. Well, can I just say, I arrived here in November of 2014 to start working at Brookings, and I was stunned by the amount of RT commercials—sorry—posters, advertisements around Washington. There were these big, expensive ones, the back-lighted ones on the bus stops, and then there were the ones that were plastered all over construction site fences. Amazing. I'd never seen anything quite like that.

So clearly, there was a big investment here directed at normal Washingtonians, and that——

Senator BLUNT. Is there no investment like that in Germany, or——

Dr. STELZENMUELLER. Not in the same way, but there is investment.

Senator BLUNT. Would you allow it if they wanted to do that?

Dr. STELZENMUELLER. You know, I tend to think that they can, if they want to buy advertisement, you know, it's a free country, okay? And these are companies. They can do this. I'm not a big fan of nanny state endeavors to protect us from things that we can perfectly well see through. And I believe that Americans can see through this as well.

Where it becomes more insidious is where they're doing covert stuff, where they're buying people, where they're buying institutions. And so I have faith——

Senator BLUNT. Your view is that's more insidious than so-called "fake news"?

Dr. STELZENMUELLER. Well, fake news is insidious if our consumers, if our citizens, are not media-literate.

Senator BLUNT. Well, let's go on down the line. Mr. Sarts, what—in other countries, what do they do about RT and other Russian outlets?

Mr. SARTS. Well, in the information space it's actually quite simple. If somebody doesn't have the credibility, they may message as much they want. There is no effect from that.

And I think there is an interesting example where Sputnik opened their offices in the Scandinavian countries, and then within a year's time they had to close it. Nobody listened to them.

Senator BLUNT. What about in Montenegro?

Ambassador GARCEVIC. Sputnik has no office in Montenegro. I think that—I barely can remember that any of those Russia-based media have offices in Montenegro itself. But they have offices in neighboring Serbia and from there they penetrate Montenegro, because they know that in the case, in the Montenegrin case, government may revoke a license at any moment. So it is not the case in Serbia. Because we speak more or less the same language, they can do that easily. And then from there, their news will be rebroadcasted or reprinted and published in Montenegro.

Senator BLUNT. And Ambassador, what, if anything, should we do about these known mediums that they use of miscommunication?

Ambassador BURNS. Senator, I think two things. One is always attach an adjective, a couple, before when we talk about them: "the Russian government propaganda station RT." So expose them for who they are, because they are Russian government.

Second, be very careful if you ever go on it, because they'll distort what you say. Don't give them the platform that they want.

Senator BLUNT. Let me try to get one more question in to you. I actually agree with your current position on Congressionally binding sanctions. I assume you were much more inclined to have a flexible position when you were at the State Department?

Ambassador BURNS. That's absolutely true. I am a creature of the Executive Branch. I always thought it's better to preserve the President's authority to act. But in this particular case, since the President is not acting, I think the Congress has to take that responsibility.

Chairman BURR. Senator King.

Senator KING. Thank you, Mr. Chairman.

Starting with just a couple of comments. One, I want to associate myself with Senator Rubio's question, which I think is the real key question of this hearing. What can we do to defend ourselves? And I'd like to ask each of you—you've already testified, talked about it—to submit a written, very short, half a page, bing, bing, bing, here are the five things that we can do to defend ourselves. I think that would be very helpful.

Secondly, what we are seeing here, it seems to me, is the invention and expansion and implementation of a new kind of warfare. And it's a kind of warfare that is particularly effective against democracies. Valeriy Gerasimov, who's the chief of the general staff of Russia, calls it "weaponizing information," and said in 2013 that he believes this is—we are engaged now in informational conflict.

Putin's defense budget is one eighth of ours, but he is playing a weak hand very well and has found a cheap way—and when I say peculiarly effective against democracies, because this is where public opinion matters. In many other countries, public opinion doesn't have that great a role in how policy is formed.

So a couple of short questions. And I think, Ambassador Burns, you just answered this. Any doubt that RT is an arm of the Russian government?

[No response.]

Senator KING. No doubt. Everybody agrees.

Secondly, I have heard in a previous hearing in a different committee that the Russians were looking around, sniffing around buying commercial TV outlets in Europe. Have any of you heard of that? Is that——

Mr. SARTS. Yes, there have been in Baltic states the cases where they've tried, but governments have tried to block these possibilities.

Senator KING. Well, that certainly it seems to me, is one of the— one of the things that we have to watch.

Another—I think this is a yes or no question. Was what was done here in 2016 absolutely consistent with what the Russians have been doing in Europe for some years? Essentially the same modus operandi? Mr.—go ahead.

Mr. SARTS. Well, it was, but there were a number of new elements and some more risk-taking than we used to see.

Senator KING. So they're getting more sophisticated. Is that that accurate?

I think, Mr. Sarts, you have said something several times that's consistent with my understanding. Some members of this Committee were in Eastern Europe over a year ago in the spring of 2016. We were in Ukraine and Poland. When we asked them how they—and the first thing they wanted to tell us is, "Watch out for the Russians in your elections." And we didn't understand how prescient that was at the time.

But in any case, then we said, "How do you defend yourself?" And the answer was, I think, exactly what you've said. They said, "The best defense is if the people know what's happening, and they can say, oh, it's just the Russians."

And that you've characterized as societal awareness, and that's what I think is one of the most important roles of this Committee, is to educate the American people that, whatever we do, whatever defenses we come up with, this is going to keep happening. And the best defense is for them to be, I think you used the word, "digitally literate," or I can't recall the term. But we need to understand that they're going to keep doing this and we need to learn to shrug it off.

Ambassador Burns, do you have any thoughts on that?

Ambassador BURNS. I much agree, and I think that's the lesson to learn from what happened to the Obama Administration. They were caught unawares. It was new. They didn't appreciate the extent of it, and it was a lack of speed and lack of transparency. That is a problem.

Senator KING. Well, but I do think it should be noted, because there's been some discussion here, they did release on October 9 a comprehensive memo that this was going on, that really listed all the elements that were later listed in the January. And in the heat of the campaign, nobody paid much attention to it. And I understand. I think the dilemma they had was, do we go public in a big way and be accused of putting our thumb on the scale of the election and those kind of things?

But I agree, I think a more aggressive response would've been—would've been appropriate in 20–20 hindsight.

One thing that hasn't been mentioned too much is the use of kompromat. Is that not part of the Russian strategy, use of salacious material against candidates they don't like? That has happened in other countries, has it not?

Dr. STELZENMUELLER. Well, it's one of the open questions about the 2015 Bundestag leak, the German federal legislature, whether they were looking for kompromat and found it. They have not posted anything yet. But, you know, that's kind of the James Bond version. They may just have—also have done this for the simple purpose of espionage. The point about kompromat is that often you don't find out because you're not supposed to.

Senator KING. Exactly.

Yes, sir?

Mr. SARTS. Just kompromat has been very heavily used typically by USSR. I think the relative importance has decreased because they've learned actually having one is not always essential. You might make it up.

Senator KING. Oh, I see. You don't even have to have the data. You can just make something up, "King Kicks Dogs Every Morning," and then I'm denying it for the next three months, or much worse.

Well, I want to thank you again for your testimony. This has been very informative and I hope you will give us some written responses about defenses because that's an important role of this Committee, to prepare ourselves for what everyone has suggested is not a one-off in 2016.

It will continue to happen and it will continue to happen on both sides of our political divide in this country. Putin is not a Republican. He is an opportunist. And the next time, this attack could come in the opposite direction, but it's still a corruption of our democracy.

Thank you all very much.

Thank you, Mr. Chairman.

Chairman BURR. Senator Lankford.

Senator LANKFORD. Thank you, Mr. Chairman. And I've learned several things today, including that Senator King kicks dogs every morning, and I was completely unaware of that.

[Laughter.]

Let me ask this panel a quick question, and it goes back to one of the heart of the questions Senator King was just bringing up before, is the deterrence. Let me ask in a more specific way: What price should Russia pay for this type of interference? It's one thing to say we're informing our people, we're trying to do it rapidly. I've heard that from several of you to say, the speed of the information and the response is exceptionally important. Finding cooperation between legitimate media sites, that they will actually help identify here's—here's false, here's true, try to get that out.

But what price should they pay? And let me bring up why. When the Russians were cheating and doping their athletes, in a very short period of time Russia paid a very big price for that by their athletes not going to the 2016 Olympics and saying, I know you trained, but you doped your athletes and you were caught for that. It's just within the last 24 hours, that their doping authority is even allowed to start testing their athletes again, they've been on suspension that long. They paid a price for that. We would hope that that would be a deterrent. What price should they pay for this type of aggression?

Yes, ma'am?

Dr. STELZENMUELLER. This is a really difficult question, politically, legally, militarily. And the main reason why it's so difficult is attribution. And even when intelligence services know how to attribute, they may not want to make that public. And that is the largest conundrum that we are dealing with here.

So we may, I think, be looking at asymmetrical retaliation, as it were, political, economic. And I think the biggest price that Russia can and should pay is failure—failure to undermine us, failure to undermine our democracies, failure to undermine our alliances. That is something we can do, and I think it is even more important because it's a consistently—it's a remaining vulnerability that is even more important than the question of retaliation.

Of course, we—and American and German and European officials have been doing this all the time, is to make it very clear to the Russians that we know what they're doing, that we want them to stop, and that we have ways of reacting.

But the actual legality and viability of symmetrical reaction is a huge legal and military problem, as I'm sure you know.

Senator LANKFORD. Yes, and one of the things you mentioned before, Dr. Stelzenmueller, is the export of LNG. That's something that was debated extensively here in Congress and a large part of that conversation was—the conversation became this is about American energy companies somehow being more profitable while the Europeans were saying this is about geopolitical power. If you don't sell us LNG, then the Russians can turn the valve on and off and they control a large part of Europe. For geopolitical influence, we need to do that. That became debated long-term here and then was finally determined, yes, we're going to sell LNG, and now Europe has another outlet and Russia has competition on it and is a benefit to our alliance and our long-term connection.

Other ideas that anyone would share as far as the price that Russia should pay?

Mr. SARTS. Well, if I may, actually one of the things that they expect us to talk soft about these things. That's kind of, you know, part of their plan: There'll not be direct, strong response. I thought when Emmanuel Macron met Putin and the way he did it in Versailles was not a pleasant experience for Putin. So, being direct, instead of what they thought will be this polite talk.

Secondly, the machinery they're using against us is extremely important for Kremlin to control their own population. So if we are able to dismantle it, then we—we actually, as I've said, we bring in more truth into the internal Russian discourse.

Senator LANKFORD. Other ideas and thoughts?

Ambassador BURNS. I would just say, Senator, it's a really tough question for both President Trump as it was for President Obama. Can we find a pressure point as important to Putin as the integrity of our elections are to us? And I think Constanze is right, that's probably going to be asymmetric.

Senator LANKFORD. Okay.

Ambassador GARCEVIC. Maybe to add a sentence, that in the introductory it was mentioned that Russia's goal is to drive a wedge between the E.U. and the U.S. I think that one of the things that must be done is that actually this Euro-Atlantic bond must exist and unity between the E.U. and the U.S. must remain. On top of what was said, asymmetric threats ask for asymmetric response.

Senator LANKFORD. Great. Thank you.

Thank you, Mr. Chairman.

Chairman BURR. Senator Manchin.

Senator MANCHIN. Thank you very much, Mr. Chairman.

And thank all of you for being here. First of all, I was very impressed in seeing our NATO allies, what all you have done in trying to thwart what Russia has done as far as meddling in your affairs. Sweden has launched a nationwide school program to teach students to identify Russian propaganda. In Lithuania, 100 citizen cyber sleuths, dubbed "elves," link up digitally to identify the feedback that people employ on social media to spread Russian disinformation. They call their daily skirmishes "elves versus trolls."

France and Britain have successfully pressured Facebook to disable tens of thousands of automated fake accounts used to sway voters close to election time, and it has doubled to 6,000 the number of monitors empowered to remove defamatory and hate filled posts.

All of this, I mean, it's amazing, I think that you all have been dealing with this. And it says here, Latvia has undertaken to ferret out clandestine Russian meddling since it broke free of the Soviet Union in 1991.

I think it goes back to what, Mr. Sarts, you just had said. They have been controlling their people by misinforming them, by basically not giving them the facts, giving them what they want them to know. When you all broke, when Latvia broke in 1991, you were able at that time to set your people free by the truth.

Have you been able to have any insurgency into Russia, getting the truth in there, using their own weapons against them, their own networks against them?

Mr. SARTS. Well, none of the governments that I know of have made a decision to do that. There are civic society groups that try to do that and bring in the different tools that might be there. Some of them—and I would argue in front of this Committee, humor, as awkward as it might be, is one of the best tools I would suggest to penetrate the control system. We in fact recently produced a report on humor as a tool of communication. In five hours since, we had a response from Maria Zakharova. And it went on for whole months, including President of Chechnya Ramzan Kadyrov doing a video as a response to our research of humor. I think that tells you a story.

So, there are many ways you can get in.

Senator MANCHIN. Okay. Let me ask this question then. There's been reports—it's open source—that Putin was directly involved giving direction in the United States elections, the last presidential election. Our intelligence basically said he was directly involved. He gave the order to do what was done. Do you have that same verification in your countries and in NATO allies that Putin was directly involved? And have you identified him as being directly involved so that people would know where it's coming from?

Dr. STELZENMUELLER. If I had that information, I probably wouldn't be sitting here. But there is a general assumption in Germany that the President's office is directly and copiously involved in giving orders to Russian interference. The actual execution is delegated very broadly to a variety of actors.

Senator MANCHIN. Anybody.

Ambassador GARCEVIC. When it comes to Montenegro, I can only repeat or quote what our state prosecutor mentioned just like a few weeks ago. He said that behind these events in Montenegro are nationalist structures from Russia and that certain Russian authorities were involved at a certain level. But we at this moment, we cannot make that conclusion that Putin himself was giving orders to what was going on there.

Senator MANCHIN. If I can follow up with one. The rhetoric coming from our White House under this Administration, has it caused our NATO allies to start moving toward contributing two percent to the defense spending? Or is it because of their concern of Russia's aggression?

We'll let all of you answer. I want Ambassador Burns too to get in on this.

Dr. STELZENMUELLER. Yes. The chancellor has said repeatedly that we will achieve the two percent by 2024, which is the date at which it was promised. And we're increasing our defense budget by 8 percent this year.

We're also doing a lot of other things which are working toward——

Senator MANCHIN. What was the cause?

Dr. STELZENMUELLER. I think the proximate cause was Russian hostility——

Senator MANCHIN. More so than the White House rhetoric?

Dr. STELZENMUELLER. I'd say that the policies and rhetoric of this Administration have been contributing to reinforcing a sense of urgency.

Senator MANCHIN. Got you. Ambassador Burns?

Ambassador BURNS. Senator, I think 20 of the 29 NATO allies have increased defense spending since the Russian invasion of Crimea and Eastern Ukraine in 2014. That was the primary cause.

But I must say, President Trump's been right to raise this issue, as all of our Presidents have. And I think he has had an impact on the internal debate. Canada is one country. They spend barely one percent of their GDP in defense. So, I think he's gone about it sometimes in a way that's not effective.

Senator MANCHIN. Unconventional.

Ambassador BURNS. Unconventional. But he's right to raise it.

Senator MANCHIN. Thank you very much.

Yes, sir.

Ambassador GARCEVIC. Just to add that last year only, other members of NATO increased defense spending by around $2 billion U.S.

Chairman BURR. Sen. Cotton.

Senator COTTON. Thank you.

This hearing has been informative on the specific question of Russian active measures in the United States and in Europe. Of course, that's just one small part of Russia's efforts over the decades to undermine Western democracies, to try to divide our alliance. I think we explored most of those points today.

So I want to respond more broadly to what I think are two myths that have been propagated here, mostly by my Democratic colleagues, but by some of these witnesses. And those myths are that somehow President Trump is weaker on Russia than was President Obama; and second, that somehow NATO and deterrence is undermined by the United States, rather than by Europe.

So first, let's review what's happened in the first five months of this Administration. President Trump has bombed the Khan Sheikhun military base in Syria. He has shot down Syrian planes. They have shot down Iranian drones, thereby showing that Russia is unable to protect its two main clients in the Middle East.

We're on the verge of deploying more troops to Afghanistan, where Russia has been meddling with ever-greater intensity in recent years. And we finally proposed a budget that increases our military spending, albeit not enough, that accelerates ballistic missile defense. And our domestic agencies are doing everything they can to promote more oil and gas production in the United States.

By contrast, President Obama famously pushed the reset button a few weeks into his tenure, six months after Russia invaded Georgia. He mocked Mitt Romney for calling Russia our number one geopolitical foe. He asked Dmitry Medvedev in a hot mic moment to wait until after the election to discuss missile defenses because he would have, quote, "more flexibility."

Despite bipartisan support in the Congress, President Obama refused to send lethal weapons to Ukraine. He stood idly by as Russia returned into the Middle East for the first time in 40 years in Syria. And he stood idly by, as we've heard today, in the 2016 election.

So, I would dispute the premise that somehow President Obama was any tougher or stronger in defense of U.S. interests as against Russia.

Second, the myth that somehow NATO and deterrence is at risk because of the United States, not Europe. Talk is cheap. Deterrence is about the military balance of power. It's not about magic words. National leaders can call Article 5 sacred or sacrosanct or inviolate or any other pretty word they want. But Europe's collective failure to meet the two percent goal of defense spending has underinvested in our common defense by something on the magnitude of $100 billion to $120 billion per year. Vladimir Putin can see the reality of what national leaders in Europe think about our common defense, no matter what words they use.

Moreover, it's well known that Russia is in flagrant violation of the Intermediate-Range Nuclear Forces Treaty. They're also in violation of the Open Skies Treaty. But European leaders continue to resist the Trump Administration's efforts to bring Russia back into compliance with those treaties.

Dr. Stelzenmueller, as you noted, the German foreign minister has protested the Russian sanctions bill that passed the Senate 97 to 2, because Germany does business with Russian companies in the construction of the Nord Stream 2 Pipeline, which by the way they shouldn't be building in the first place if they are that worried about Russia and want to deter Russia in Europe.

While we're on the topic of the German foreign minister, he said a few months ago that the 2 percent goal is unlikely to be obtained and politicians shouldn't make promises they can't keep. Sadly, I'm afraid he's right. Germany increased its budget last year by 8 percent. This year its defense budget is proposed to be increased by only 4 percent, yet a Forza Agency poll suggested that a majority of Germans oppose such an increase.

More alarmingly, a Pew poll from last month asked Europeans: If Russia got into a serious military conflict with one of its neighboring countries that is our NATO ally, do you think our country should or should not use military force to defend that country? Here were their responses. The Dutch said, 72 percent yes, 23 percent no. That is great for the Dutch. They are good allies. Poles, 62 to 26; Americans 62 to 31—by a 2 to 1 margin, very proud of our country. Canada, 56—58 to 31; France, 53 to 43; Spain, 46 to 46—not great. Brits, 45 to 43. Germans, 40 to 53 would defend a NATO ally.

So my time is almost expired. I'll just ask one question. Given that so many of my remarks have focused on Germany and, Dr. Stelzenmueller, you're obviously the subject matter expert on that country, what is the matter with Germany?

Dr. STELZENMUELLER. Thank you, Senator, for your questions and for your remarks. I've already said that I am not a fan of the Nord Stream 2 project, and I think a number of many of my German experts, friends, agree with me. There is a substantial debate within German politics about the use of this project, politically.

On the German defense budget, I think, again—I can only reiterate what Chancellor Merkel has said, who looks likely to win this election again, that Germany is on course to fulfill this promise by the time it is supposed to fulfill it. Anybody who has ever looked at defense budgets and attempted to increase them knows how many past dependencies, complications, there are in actually expanding forces. We would have to double our defense budget to do this.

But I can assure you from my personal experience, many conversations last week in Berlin, we are racing to do this. In fact, only last week—or two weeks ago, I was on the stage in Koblenz together with the German chairman of the chief—the equivalent of the chairman of the joint chiefs, at the bidding of the Defense Ministry, to explain to Germany's armament bureaucracies why they have to work faster, more flexibly, and more creatively to accomplish the promises that we have made to NATO. And I assure you that this was a very serious discussion.

Now, it will also not have escaped you, because we've been talking about this all day, that we're in an election, and that Gabriel is a member of the opposite party, although he is in a coalition with the chancellor, and therefore he has to say these things. He has also said other things. For example, the first time he went to

Moscow he told Foreign Minister Lavrov, his counterpart, that he did not believe in the post-Western world Lavrov had spoken of in that Munich Security Conference, that this was wrong, that we very much stand by the idea of the Western—of the West and Western alliances, and that this is a question of shared values and not of geopolitical location.

So, as for the Pew poll, I'm as unhappy about that as you are and I know many Germans who are unhappy about it as well. Maybe that is also rooted in our cultural memory of the Cold War. I am old enough to remember the Cold War, where we knew that if the Article 5 came to pass, there would be three weeks of conventional warfare, then it would move to nuclear, and then my country would be a heap of ashes. I think that that is a memory that informs that kind of judgment.

But I know that German politicians of all parties have made it clear beyond a shadow of a doubt to Russia, to Moscow, and to the Kremlin and Mr. Putin himself that any violation of Article 5 will have us all standing there as one, as allies, to defend an attack on NATO territory.

Chairman BURR. Senator Harris.

Senator HARRIS. Ambassador Burns, can you tell me what you believe has been the impact on our reputation with our allies, in Europe in particular, as a result of this Administration's failure to acknowledge that Russia hacked and attempted to manipulate the election of the President of the United States? And if you believe there has been an impact in terms our standing with our allies in Europe, do you believe that it's going to have an impact on our ability to protect ourselves and guard against what should be a predictable attack in our 2018 elections by Russia?

Ambassador BURNS. Thank you, Senator. I think the basic problem is that the Europeans are accustomed to looking toward—for the United States to lead on any big issue. This is a big issue, and the hearing is central to it, because all of us are under attack from a systematic Russian campaign. But they don't see the United States leading.

And if you combine—and this is partly in response to Senator Cotton's very good question as well. President Trump has not been strong on the sanctions against Ukraine. He's not an advocate for the territorial independence of Ukraine. He's not spoken out on interference and he's been very ambivalent, even hostile, to NATO, and seems to look at Germany as a strategic economic competitor, not as an ally.

If you put all that together, I think it is the first time since 1945 that Europeans might likely see Angela Merkel right now as leader of the West, not President Trump. I don't say that lightly and I think it's a sad statement to make, but I think it's a true statement. And so we need to recover our leadership role, and you do that by actions.

And on this subject, it's by aligning yourself with the Europeans on the sanctions issue. That's why I support what the Senate has done on a bipartisan basis. And it's by trying to raise our defenses, as Janis has talked about here, in a very effective way.

Senator HARRIS. And can any of the other panelists offer that?

Mr. Chairman and Vice Chairman, I appreciate you having this hearing and an open hearing on the issue. I think the American people should have a better sense of how our reputation and standing in the global community has been impacted by our failure to acknowledge that Russia attempted to manipulate an election for the President of the United States.

Do any of the other panelists want to add to the Ambassador's point?

Ambassador GARCEVIC. I will add, just to remind you that the Article 5 has been invoked only once in the history of NATO, in the situation when the U.S. was under attack after September 11th, and that all our allies from Europe stood up and stand behind U.S. at that time. And we've been in Afghanistan for years now together, alongside, fighting the same cause.

Dr. STELZENMUELLER. I'll just add one number to that. More than 800 Europeans have died alongside American troops fighting in Afghanistan, for a joint cause.

Senator HARRIS. Thank you.

Mr. Sarts, you mentioned a couple of points about the French elections. And I was curious about—and Senator Collins I think raised this point also—you talked about media as a partner and their cooperation with the French government, and that they actually were very active in verifying the factual accuracy of misinformation.

You also discussed the importance of assuming that a country will be hacked and then trapping hackers, and arguably then at some point being able to prosecute them in France and get some consequence and accountability.

How would you propose that that would be applied in the United States? You know that, for example, I won't name the stations, but there are two cable networks that if you watch them at the same time on the same subject, you will hear two completely different versions of what's happening. And so we have to acknowledge that we have a culture around the media in this country as it relates to politics at least that may not be as coordinated as some of the media in Europe.

How would you propose—again looking at the 2018 election as a goal for protecting ourselves, how would we work with the media to inoculate or prevent harm or to be resilient once we know we've been hacked?

Mr. SARTS. Well, truth and facts matter. Facts matter. We don't build bridges on false facts. We want to then get them straight. It is very hard to have a functional democracy without facts as a basis for it.

We tend to go into different directions because of opinions, and that's okay. That's what the democratic process is. But at the end of the day, all we have to agree is that if we don't value the factual basis of our reality, democracy would not work.

Senator HARRIS. I'm sorry, I only have a couple of seconds. How did the French media expose a misstatement of fact to be without factual basis? How did they expose the fake news, if you will? What did they do?

Mr. SARTS. There are a whole set of ways how you verify what the information is in front of them. The journalists should be very good at it. And actually, the whole—the biggest point is actually value and understand the role, as it is called, soft power. It is both also the power and the responsibility. And understand that within the responsibility of that for media in a democratic society, to have it functional is to value the factual basis. That's I think the understanding upon which the French media were able to come together to actually work together.

I wouldn't classify there was a cooperation between media and the government. Media cooperated in between themselves irrespective of different political viewpoints, valuing that the democratic system is based on fact.

Senator HARRIS. I agree with that. And I would just say that it's important to value a free and independent press in order to allow them to do their job. Thank you.

Chairman BURR. Senator McCain.

Senator MCCAIN. Mr. Garcevic, do you believe that the United States has a strategy to respond to the cyber warfare that we're in today?

Ambassador GARCEVIC. I think yes.

Senator MCCAIN. Could you tell me that strategy?

Ambassador GARCEVIC. That's a very difficult question. I would say that I can see that strategy through NATO and what I also——

Senator MCCAIN. Through NATO?

Ambassador GARCEVIC. Yes, because when it comes to cyber attacks, you remember that as a result of the first cyber attack on a large scale, which happened years ago when Russia attacked Estonia, a Center of Excellence was established in Estonia, which was supposed to be——

Senator MCCAIN. That didn't have anything to do with an American strategy. I was there at the opening of it.

Ambassador GARCEVIC. Yes, but I think that there is a—in our case, in our case, if I can just return to our case, you know, thanks to—when we found out that it would be difficult, at least as far as I know, it would be difficult to clarify the case, we turned to and asked for help from the U.S. and the U.K. agencies.

I would like to believe that, you know, that strategy exists. I can only—I cannot comment on it because I'm not—I'm not in the loop. I didn't read it. I didn't talk to people who can explain. But what I can see that's happening every day there is that through your embassies and through your diplomatic network, a network that exists in NATO at the working level, countries like Montenegro if in need receive assistance.

Senator MCCAIN. Well, that's a great answer. Thank you.

Should we expect similar aggressive behavior as we saw in the attempt to overthrow the government of Montenegro at other NATO aspirants, such as Bosnia and Herzegovina, Macedonia, Kosovo?

Ambassador GARCEVIC. What I mentioned in my introductory, I'm sure that this is just one case and I'm sure that Russia will continue doing something similar in our neighborhood.

Senator MCCAIN. That's pretty exciting. They recruited people. They were——

Ambassador GARCEVIC. Yes.

Senator MCCAIN [continuing]. Willing to kill people. They were willing to send people in uniform to kill the Prime Minister. I mean, it's—it reads out of a novel.

Ambassador GARCEVIC. That's why I think that U.S. and European partners must remain active in the region. And if there were any retreat from the region would be detrimental for democracies in our part of——

Senator MCCAIN. They came awfully close to succeeding. If we hadn't had an informant from the inside, they might have succeeded.

Ambassador GARCEVIC. What I answered—what I answered previously, that in some cases we simply hit luck. I cannot say that we were capable to fight back. Simply it happened as a result of certain circumstances. One of them you mentioned. And that helped us a lot.

Senator MCCAIN. Like an informant on the inside.

Ambassador GARCEVIC. Yes, this was an informant who came to—who was aware of the proportion of bloodshed that would happen if this action succeeded. And he turned to—he turned and showed up in police to report.

Senator MCCAIN. Mr. Sarts, should we be concerned about that level of violence that the GRU is willing to engage in in order to overthrow a freely elected government?

Mr. SARTS. It is concerning and we should be concerned.

Senator MCCAIN. Why do you think we haven't heard more about it?

Mr. SARTS. I'm quite surprised about that as well, because I think that is a very, very telling story that we have to reflect upon.

I have one hope, and that is the fact that it all failed. Russians, like everybody else, do their lessons learned. So I hope the lesson that they learned, it's not really that effective. And in these cases, they tend to lose what they like to have, that is plausible deniability, at least——

Senator MCCAIN. What has been publicly actioned in Montenegro about this failed coup?

Ambassador GARCEVIC. I would say reaction was mixed, even including me, at the beginning. I was at that time in the U.S., not working any more for government. And the first reaction was a mix of feelings, whether this was staged or not, whether it is true or not.

But time goes on and we are more and more aware of the proportion of the action and what was behind this action and how the action was organized. And then, also, as a result of two suspects decided to cooperate with the police and they disclosed in their verdicts how action was planned, who financed it, who were the people for contacts in Serbia, those two agents that I mentioned at the beginning.

Senator MCCAIN. What—go ahead.

Ambassador GARCEVIC. The Russian agents. Then this actually helped us make this picture completed, putting pieces one by one so then now we have clear picture what was happening——

Senator MCCAIN. What's the reaction in the Baltics, Mr. Sarts?

Mr. SARTS. In the Baltics, I think currently all the governments are looking at—there's a great concern at the big-scale Russian military exercise that is planned for September, Zapad 2017. We, from all——

Senator MCCAIN. Are you talking about the reaction to what was clearly a very complex, detailed plot to violently overthrow a freely elected government?

Mr. SARTS. Well, there were all kinds of political statements condemning that. There was a discussion within the countries, both—within the government's closed circles as well as openly, of what has been the parameters of it. And I would tell that governments have taken very great care to look into elements of what made it, and what was the plan, to make adjustments for their own planning in the case of this particular crisis.

Senator MCCAIN. I thank you, Mr. Chairman.

Chairman BURR. Senator Reed.

Senator REED. Well, thank you very much, Mr. Chairman.

Thank you, panel, for an excellent discussion. Ambassador Burns, thank you for your distinguished service to the country in so many ways, and your wise counsel. And thank you for promoting us to the best hope of fixing this problem. But I think we're the second best, frankly. I share your concern that the President really has to take the lead here for obvious reasons. Commander-in-chief, chief diplomat, the most recognized public figure.

There was a missed opportunity at the NATO conference. Forget what was said. What wasn't said was the common threat we face today, the most significant one, not the only one, is this deliberate action by the Russians.

And my sense at least, that the most immediate game changer would be if the President, standing next to the Chancellor and to the President of France and to the British Prime Minister, took that position. I assume you might have an opinion on that.

Ambassador BURNS. Well, I do. I was Ambassador to NATO, as you know, Senator. And every American President has been the leader of that alliance, has affirmed that bedrock commitment. And we know it was in the President's speech and it came out, and so it had a devastating impact on American leadership.

What we haven't talked about today is that, in addition to the intelligence and judicial and political measures to take to defend against the interference in our elections, you and Chairman McCain lead another Committee. We have to keep funding the rebuilding of the U.S. military in Europe; I hope permanently station the NATO battalions in Estonia, Latvia, Lithuania and Poland, because we're into containment of Russian power. We're back into containment on multiple levels. And this hearing exposes one of those levels.

Senator REED. In that spirit, though, not only the reaffirmation of Article 5, but also a positive statement about the common threat of cyber against the United States. We missed one opportunity, but if the President could stand with the leadership of NATO and the Prime Minister of Canada and many other interested parties and make that declaration, that would do as much to stop this process as anything. Is that fair?

Ambassador BURNS. Well, it would, because the immediate threat now is this threat. It's the cyber attacks on the electoral processes. It's a much bigger threat than the conventional threat.

He has the opportunity. He'll be in Germany the week after next. He'll be at a summit hosted by Chancellor Merkel. There are opportunities for the President to get back into this leadership role and to try to build some bridges with the European leaders.

My sense is that Secretary Tillerson and Secretary Mattis want us to go in that direction. They've been talking publicly about trying to play a bigger leadership role, a more concerted one.

Senator REED. Well, thank you.

Mr. Sarts, we have had discussions about the vulnerabilities of our electoral system, our information, social media, all of these things. We know, as several people have suggested, that they're coming back.

From your perspective, are the Russians working on—you know, already working on, in our case the 2016 campaign and the 2018 campaign in the United States? Are they going to deploy more sophisticated cyber operations against our registration and electoral systems?

There's been some reports, in Great Britain, within the context of the Brexit vote, that there was an attack on registration systems. And, I guess the biggest question of them all is, are they already there and we don't know it because of the ability to use some tools that have fallen into their hands? So, if you could.

Mr. SARTS. One thing that we've registered, Russians do experimentation. Sometimes you see an odd pattern that is inconsequential in the given circumstances and you kind of dismiss it because it has no effect. But when you look forward or retrospectively when you see these cases, you see that has been the test case for a particular tool.

So they're doing it right now. It's not necessarily that they test it in the theater they're going to deploy it. It might be a very different place. So, yes, there will be elaborate—more elaborate tools, both from technical, but also from a cognitive perspective. I would expect there'll be more. But I think the choices whether to and how to do that would be made pretty close within the contextual circumstances of the moment.

Senator REED. Now, your Center for Strategic Communication, are you actually dealing with this issue of, in Germany, for example, the upcoming election, trying to help them in the United States, trying to give advice? Is NATO taking the position, with we hope U.S. leadership, of proactively dealing with this? Or are you caught up in this kind of paralysis that we see in the United States?

Mr. SARTS. Well, NATO is facing now this from a very different—well, not very, but slightly different angle, where the NATO is putting troops in the three Baltics and Poland. They are bombarded with disinformation, with fake news. Robotic networks are trying to attack. So NATO is taking different trends of response, capability build-up, practical steps, etcetera, etcetera.

We at the Center, we are not part of the military structure. We are run by the countries that made our Center, so we respond to them; and if they ask, and they do, to give our advice, knowledge, or methodology, how they can counter specific cases, including election, we are there to support them.

Senator REED. Thank you very much.

My time is expired. Thank you all very much.

Chairman BURR. Thank you, Senator Reed.

Thank you to all members for their participation today. And more importantly, thank you to each and every one of you. Your expertise is invaluable to us. Your testimony today is crucial, as I shared with all of you before this panel, at our ability not only to work through the current investigation that we're in, but to create a road map for the appropriate committees of jurisdiction, both at home to figure out how we can change elections to build defensive mechanisms or to make it less vulnerable and to work globally with our partners to make sure that any changes, any best practices might at least be shared and offered to be implemented.

Just a couple of comments I've got. I was challenged from the beginning with the names today. I remain as challenged trying to figure out exactly what we do to stop Russian interference. But as we complete this process, I think we'll have a clearer and clearer picture.

You've been asked today to submit some things. I would also ask you to think about the challenges that we've got and that you have in your respective areas of expertise and provide any additional input to us that you feel is pertinent to the decisions we'll make.

Ambassador Burns, again I go back to something that you said and it's what Jim Comey said: Next time it could be the other party. As a matter of fact, when this whole effort started it wasn't targeted at one party or the other. I know you know that because you know the root of when this started, and it was a mere phishing expedition that probably encompassed hundreds, if not thousands, of individuals and nonprofits and organizations.

It turned into a data-rich environment for Russia to be involved in an election. No question they would have been involved, but maybe not in the same direct way. They just happened to have accumulated the data. So right at the heart of it is this cyber security issue that the world continues to deal with and try to figure out what the silver bullet is. And the answer is there's not a silver bullet.

The second thing is, I'm glad you admit it: You are a product of the State Department. And, you know, I can't envision the day that there would be a Secretary of any State Department that would be in favor of sanctions from the U.S. to a foreign entity because it's inherent that that makes their job tougher.

But even though I don't think Secretary Tillerson is out there calling for Russian sanctions, I wouldn't expect any Secretary to do it. But there has to be—there has to be leadership. And I think that's what the world's crying for right now, is for leadership. And I hope that we do what we have historically done and we fill that vacuum, not because we're better at it. It's because I think as I travel the world, the world's waiting for us to do it because we provide a liability umbrella for a lot of countries. Because our elections have certainty and most other elections don't have the length of time certainty that we do.

So there are things that are unique to the United States and we have to realize how that aids our partners around the world at leveraging that certainty of U.S. elections.

So here's where I end up. I believe voters in Asheville, North Carolina and Houston, Texas deserve the same thing and that's to vote with no interference. Just as voters in Berlin and Paris deserve elections that have confidence that their votes and the integrity of their election systems are intact.

As the Committee continues its investigation, it's increasingly clear that Russian activities fell into what I would refer to as a seam. It was domestic activity by a foreign power, so the intelligence community wasn't quite sure how to approach it. It involved what I might informally call pseudo-government, organizations and the political party, so that it confused our government's approach somewhat.

Lastly, the intelligence community diligently avoids political issues. So that added to the additional complexity of this problem.

Here's where we are today. This Committee's got a charge from the leadership and that's to thoroughly review Russia's meddling in the 2016 election. And the Committee has committed to finish that investigation no matter how long it takes, no matter what the results are.

I'm not sure that Russia's involvement in our election will change much from our initial assessment, which was the ICA that was produced by the Obama Administration. But what this Committee can do and should do is to make sure that every American and every person globally that cares about the integrity of elections, reviews what we find, embraces what's needed to assure that elections are fair and there's no interference in the future, and that we collectively commit to make sure that we carry that out.

So the Committee's work is vitally important to how this difficult time in our history ends. But I'm confident that we can come out of this with a report that not only spells it out for those of us that are members of Congress, but spells it out for the American people and our partners abroad in a way that can be understood and can be received with confidence.

Your contribution today has been incredibly helpful to our ability to put that report together.

With that, this hearing is adjourned.

[Whereupon, at 12:40 p.m., the hearing was adjourned.]